My Friend Sam
Esther L. Roberts

Kind and Creative, LLC

Copyright © 2018 by **Esther L. Roberts**

All rights reserved. No part of this publication may be reproduced, distributed or transmitted in any form or by any means, without prior written permission from the author: esther@appalachianchic.com

Kind and Creative, LLC
8216 Strawberry Plains Pike
Knoxville, Tennessee 37924
www.kindandcreativellc.com

My Friend Sam/Esther L. Roberts -- 1st edition
ISBN 978-0-578-40423-3

for Sam

Acknowledgements

Thank you to everyone who knew and loved Sam and encouraged me to write this book. And thanks to everyone who reads, comments, and shares my articles—you inspire me every day and I feel blessed by each one of you.

Thank you to my mother, Gretchen. Your support of my love for Sam gave me twenty-six years of joy and happiness and a lifetime of perfect memories.

Thank you to my sister, Frankie, who inspires me daily with her unparalleled authenticity and faith in God. It is my greatest life privilege to have you as my sister and my friend.

Thank you to Terri and Doug Reece, David and Sadie Stroud, and Doris S. Grayson. At different points in my life, y'all helped me provide a home and/or food for Sam when I was going through some dark, lonely valleys of life. Without your kindness, my journey with Sam may not have been a 'happily ever after.' I can never repay your generosity.

Thank you to Libbi Moir and her family, who welcomed me and Sam into their family for Sam's golden years and supported me through the soul-shattering loss of my best friend.

Thank you to Cathy Keeton, my friend, soul sister, and outstanding horsewoman, riding instructor, and trainer. It is my privilege to call you "teacher" and "friend."

A special note of thanks to Katrina Love Senn, who has supported my personal journey and inspired me to find my voice as a writer, value my own self, and enjoy a life path of unending growth and inspiration.

Finally, my special and heartfelt thanks to Lady Eleanor Grace Roberts and to Kaliwohi; they continue to teach me that life goes on and love can grow again. Grace with her spirit, elegance, and bottomless "try," and Kaliwohi with his strength and doting affection—truly, I have been incredibly blessed to have not one but three perfect horses share my life.

Truly, my cup runneth over (Psalm 23:5).

God bless the animals, and each of us, as well.

Esther

Prologue

My first full-sized truck was a three-quarter ton flatbed Chevrolet that had obviously made its way down to a used car lot in Tennessee after several hard winters up north. The running boards were long gone and the lower half of the cab and doors resembled rusty Swiss cheese. The flatbed, once solid white oak, was now a splintery termite buffet. The upside was that one needn't crawl beneath the bed to inspect the rear axle; all you had to do was look between the boards. The first gear to fail in an automatic transmission is usually reverse. You crank the engine and drop the gearshift into "R."

And absolutely nothing happens.
You can rev the engine to 6,000 rpms but the tranny won't catch and the truck just sits. The remedy is to physically push the truck backward until you can utilize a forward gear. Or never park where you can't pull forward.

I was in grad school at the time, studying piano at the University of Tennessee. I remember one crisp, autumn night in the parking lot behind the music building. I was wearing a long-sleeved white blouse and a black floor-length skirt, typical accompanist attire, right down to my 2" heels—the perfect height for nuanced pedaling on a Steinway D. As I recollect, the gig that night was a solo bassist in his junior recital. It was late, I was tired, and I climbed into the cab of that truck hoping against hope that Chevy would give me reverse.

The engine howled as I revved that truck, but there was only one way out of the parking space. So I dropped the gearshift into neutral, climbed out of the cab, walked around to the mottled used-to-be-chrome grill, and pushed. Five-foot-two pianist versus a couple tons of Detroit's finest. "Stubborn" is the taproot of my family tree.

Slowly, that rusty flatbed started to roll backward. Like an old ship leaving dry dock, the truck slowly emerged out of the parking space. As it rolled, it picked up momentum. And there were parked cars all around.

Generally speaking, when I'm standing straight up, fully erect, I can barely see over the hood of most pickups. Given the task at hand, I was hunched down and hell-bent on pushing that truck. It wasn't until I realized I was no longer *pushing* that I knew I had another problem.

Across the parking lot, clean and shiny, was an Audi station wagon. The streetlights made the sleek white car glimmer in the darkness. And the rear bumper of my "bondo special" had a two inch ball on a four inch drop hitch aimed right for the driver's side door of that pristine import. Grabbing my skirt up around my knees, I sprinted alongside my runaway flatbed, praying for mercy. Like the slow-motion replay of a bad movie clip, I watched my hand reach out to the cab and sling open the door. I grabbed the wheel and catapulted into the driver's seat, smashing both feet against the brake pedal, as the Audi grew larger-than-life in the rearview mirror.

My Friend Sam

They say God takes care of fools and children. I'm not sure who "they" are, exactly, but I do believe that God takes care of young girls who drive old trucks. I threw my truck into "park" and stepped around to the rear. In the glow of the streetlights, I could just make out the rusty hitch and ball, one inch shy of skewering that Audi.

My old pickup went through more than one rebuilt transmission over the course of time, and I went through a couple more modest means of transportation, including a 4-cylinder pickup that was so "stripped down" it did not have a radio or air conditioning, but the day finally arrived when I decided to buy a brand new, full-sized pickup.

My grandfather was the main male in my life as a child, and I still respected his opinion when it came time to buy a new truck. Born in 1900, he had seen ninety-six summers the year I went "dream truck" shopping, but his mind was still sharp, just like his tongue.

Grandpa sat me down and said, "If you are going to sign your name to a note in order to buy a vehicle, you need to do three things. First, get *exactly* what you want—do not compromise—or you'll wind up trading it in and having to start all over again (sound advice for choosing a spouse, too, I've since learned, but I digress). Second, pay it off as quickly as you can. Third, take excellent care of it—change the oil, rotate the tires, fix little things before they become big things. You take care of that truck, and it'll take care of you."

Despite the years I had driven a Chevy (or perhaps because of this), I had no brand loyalty, so I went around to all the local dealerships and looked at all the makes and models. Grandpa *didn't* go with me.

"Your loan. Your business."

There were no GMCs of the right size to be found, "but we can order one for you, little lady." Yeah. Right.

The 1996 Chevy seats were designed for a hunchback—I felt curled up into a ball. The Dodge dash was so high I could hardly see over it! In 1996, trucks were built to fit the Marlboro Man and nobody ever dreamed that one day some folks might consider a neon-colored four-door vehicle with a four-foot-by-four-foot box tacked behind the cab that can carry exactly three bags of mulch for some weekend yupiecowboywannabe—as being considered a *truck*. That's just an El Camino on steroids.

Over on the local Ford lot, I spied a '96 F250. Seven and a half liter V-8. Four hundred and sixty horses. Extended cab, long bed, off-road 4x4 suspension with towing package. Dark teal with grey interior. Eleven miles. *Eleven.* Even the engine block smelled new. With the slight modification of a pillow stuffed under a t-shirt over the driver's seatback, even vertically-challenged me could both see over the dash and reach the pedals just fine.

Grandpa insisted I learn to handle the new truck in all sorts of tight spots. His philosophy? "If you can't drive it, *park it!*" Then he'd wink and add, "And if you can't park it, drive a car.

"Change up the engine speed for the first thousand miles to break the engine in so it runs well at any speed." So I logged some stop-and-go city driving, some winding back roads, some interstate miles. Five miles at fifty-five miles per hour. Five at sixty-five. Up to seventy-five. Back down to fifty-five. Push up to eighty. Down to sixty-two. Up to seventy-eight. Down to fifty. Five miles at a time, with all four-hundred-and-sixty horses teasing me the whole time.

The odometer had passed fifteen hundred miles before I pegged that 460 for the first time. The sheer joy of a fine machine running flat out made my heart sing and I laughed out loud as the countryside roared by in a blur. Fortunately, neither Grandpa nor any state troopers were on that particular stretch of Tennessee back road that day.

Did I mention God takes care of girls who drive trucks?

Chapter One

The first word I ever spoke was "pony." It's written right there in my baby book, between the typical naked-baby-in-the-crib photograph page and the section marked "Pre-School." Somewhere along the way I also learned to say "Mama," which, as with many Southern children, turned quickly into, "Mommie," and to this day it still brings a smile to that lady's face if I sign a card "to Mommie." I also learned how to say, "Daddy," but I rarely ever used that word. These days, "paternal dna" is the closest I can come.

But "pony" was my first word, and I remember asking for a pony every Christmas and every birthday to anyone and everyone who would listen: Santa Claus at the old Miller's department store with the appropriately cherry red glazed brick exterior up on Henley Street in Knoxville; the Easter Bunny, too, when he came to the same store. Sit and get your picture made. Fine. I'll smile for the camera, despite being terrified of bearded men in red suits and weirdly human-shaped rabbits with worn-out fabric on the tips of his ears. Just bring me my pony, please, and don't hold on to me for one second longer than necessary to take the picture.

In fairness to my child's heart, I never asked for a *perfect* pony. My mind never dreamed of snow-white ponies with polished black hoofs. There were no fantasies of flawless, flowing manes and tails festooned with pink ribbons. No, my mind's eye saw a much more modest mount. Perhaps a scruffy, tawny Shetland pony, like the one who lived next door. Maybe he was even for sale? His name was pathetic: "Has Been."

Has Been's owners were very kind neighbors and, once I was big enough, they taught me to bridle and saddle Has Been and I could ride whenever I liked. Well, I could *try* to ride. Has Been had notions of his own about when *he* liked to give rides. Most days were not good days to ride in Has Been's opinion. He would hold his breath to inflate his belly so no amount of effort could get the cinch straps tight enough. As soon as my foot stepped into the stirrup, "whoof!" he would let out all that air and the saddle would slip to his side. I'd have to start saddling him all over again. Loosen the twisted cinch straps. Pull off the saddle. Straighten the saddle blanket. Put the saddle back on. Race to tighten the cinch straps before Has Been could fill his entire body with air. Hot Air Has Been. That's what his name should have been.

Sometimes I dreamed of a pinto pony—shiny black spots on a sparkling white coat. Or maybe a red pony like the one in that book. But that was a sad story and I wanted a happy horse. Or pony. Size didn't matter. Neither did color.

Livestock was not allowed on our lot. Our house was on a corner, the last house inside the city limits. We were in a subdivision, if you could call it that. Somebody had subdivided a large farm years ago, so I guess that's what made folks call it a subdivision. But it was certainly a *rural* subdivision. There were no building codes, no limited set of

My Friend Sam

floorplan options, no sidewalks anywhere. And there were narrow, winding country roads all around. Across a tiny single-lane street on one side of our lot, just across the city limit line, lived Has Been with his family. Directly in front of our house was Wheeler Street. Wheeler Street was the equivalent of an asphalt slalom course and the natives took it like the avid NASCAR fans they were. It didn't matter if it was a Mustang or an old clunker, everyone went zooming downhill, straightening out the curves by completely disregarding the dingy double yellow line, as well as any oncoming traffic. It was never a good idea to chase a stray ball if it wandered out of the front yard.

Across Wheeler Street, however, was my idea of heaven. Those neighbors had horses! Not ponies like Has Been—*horses*. The land was nothing more than a scrabbly, barren holler, with a couple of strands of rusty barbed wire strung on hand-hewn cedar posts. But who cared? Behind that rickety fence, standing proud on the dusty, grassless slopes was Prince, the mahogany bay saddle horse, and Lynn, the smallish round piebald mare. They were owned by Buddy and Pat. Buddy, like Prince, was tall and lean. Pat was a petite lady, tough as nails yet gentle as a spring breeze. Pat could launch herself, unaided, onto Lynn's bare back. Pat was the finest horsewoman I'd ever seen.

Buddy and Pat were always kind and good neighbors, and they often invited me to come over and pet Prince and Lynn. Buddy would watch at his driveway until there were no cars coming, and then he'd say, "Okay! Come on!" and I'd dash across Wheeler Street, eager to pet a velvet nose and scratch a dusty ear.

Buddy taught me how to brush a horse and follow the swirls and whorls. "Stroke in the same direction the hair grows," he would say. If he ever heard me whispering, "I wish you were mine, Prince," or "maybe someday, Lynn," he never told me to hush. We both knew it was nothing more than the fantasies of a ten-year-old girl. I could never afford a horse of my own.

My parents divorced when I was six years old. That was a scandal in our little town, because back then, nice ladies didn't divorce, even if their husbands were drunken, abusive philanderers. It just wasn't proper. And there was me and my two older sisters to raise. But enough was enough, and getting rid of my paternal dna was the second-best gift my mother ever gave me.

We had some lean years, sure enough. An elementary schoolteacher's salary was hardly enough to feed and clothe three children, pay a mortgage, a car payment, the light bill, etcetera and etcetera. Those "etceteras" must have been overwhelming to my mother, bless her hardworking heart. In my youth, I only knew I wore hand-me-down clothes from my sisters, and the faded colors embarrassed me whenever I stood next to my classmates for the annual class picture. I hated having to carry a paper sack lunch while my classmates ate pizza and cheeseburgers from the school cafeteria. I resented the warning that came as my sack lunch was made for me each morning: "Bring back that paper sack so we can use it again tomorrow." A paper sack lasts at least a month, so long as you don't spill anything on it.

My mother did the very best she could, and sometimes she seemed to make miracles happen. I remember one Christmas when I woke up to find a brand new palomino paint rocking horse beside the Christmas tree! In hindsight, I hate to think what my sisters did without that year so mother could spend every spare penny on that rocking horse. It was the closest she could come to making my one dream become a reality. I logged hundreds of hours "galloping" on that spring-action plastic horse. If I mounted from the left side, his name was, "Thunder." If I hopped on from the right, I called him "Lightning."

By the time I was twelve, I had stopped asking for a pony. I knew better. My sisters and I got one bag of jellybeans, split three ways, for Easter, along with tiny, waxy white-chocolate bunnies. Christmas was a coconut to share, one orange apiece, a handful of cheap chocolate, and a new flannel nightgown that she had stayed up until the wee hours of Christmas morning to finish and wrap, using bows from prior years that stuck just fine with a fresh piece of Scotch tape.

Every Christmas after the divorce, one member of the local Masonic chapter would come to the house and bring each of us girls a present. He always brought a brand new gift, one for each of us, still in the cellophane box from Emery's 5 & 10-cent store, wrapped with shiny festive paper with a fresh bow. My mother was a devoted member of the Order of the Eastern Star, as was her mother, and my grandfather had been a Mason all his life. Politics and "The Da Vinci Code" aside, the Masons have always been extremely good to me and my family.

One year, my "Mason's gift" was a beautiful bay stallion, a plastic model I had admired for weeks at Emery's. I cherished that model then. I still do. That modest piece of plastic serves as a fond remembrance of a noble gentleman's efforts to bring some happiness to innocent children in a small Tennessee town. I hope that Mason, resting now in his eternal home, knows how very much he succeeded.

Chapter Two

One Saturday morning, Buddy pulled up with an old red--and-white horse trailer hitched to his truck. With the added length of the trailer, he couldn't turn easily into his own driveway, so he parked in ours. I was out the front door before he came to a complete stop. As Buddy climbed out of his truck, I heard an eager whinny from inside the horse trailer. Sure enough, Buddy had bought a new horse!

Prince and Lynn were pacing the fence and whinnying, and from inside the horse trailer came a trumpeted response. As Buddy opened the trailer doors, an awkward, fuzzy colt backed out. He was hardly more than a yearling, with the spiky mane and broomish tail that comes from having baby hair mixed in with the new growth toward adulthood. The colt was a skewbald pinto. God had started with a dark sorrel red horse and dipped him in white paint up to his knees, front and rear. With a careless brush, He had painted a white "T" on the colt's forehead and spattered white droplets all down his nose. Then, apparently not wanting to waste His white paint, God poured the rest of it over the colt's shoulders. On his left side, the colt was white all across his shoulder and elbow, and leg all the way down. One his right shoulder, however, like the Red Sea, God had parted the white paint to create a large spot the shape of Africa and the color of Tennessee red clay.

Buddy walked the new horse up and down our driveway and I drank in every detail as the colt readjusted his balance on the non-moving ground. He was small and scrawny like some tweenage boy who couldn't consume enough daily calories, and he moved with the gracelessness of a juvenile. Even at his young age, however, it was evident his bloodlines included stock horses of some type. His head bore the wedge shape typical of the American Quarter Horse, yet he lacked their breadth of chest and muscular build. His legs were thick-boned and his neck was short and straight. His ears were small and well defined. His eyes were large and dark. They reflected the confusion he was feeling at the moment—anxious in unfamiliar surroundings, curious about the random tufts of grass that grew amongst the grey limestone gravel of our driveway, modest rebellion at the lead rope that kept him from roaming where he would.

"His name is Sam."

A horse named Sam. Sam the horse. Sam, the red, white, gangly, small, young, untrained horse. Samuel means, literally, "God has heard." Divine.

Having devoured every book in the local library on horses over the years, I was confident as I approached young Sam to pet him for the first time. *Let a new equine acquaintance smell you first,* the pages instructed, *and always keep your fingers together, palm up and hand flat.*

Sam sniffed my outstretched hand, searching for a treat. He opened his mouth and Buddy cautioned, "Don't let him bite you!" Sam the horse, however, behaved more like Sam the dog, as he pushed his tongue into my hand and began to methodically lick the salt off my sweaty palm. His tongue was long and pink and sticky wet with horse slobber, but I didn't mind.

I raised my other hand and let Sam lick the sweat off that palm, too. Lazily, he stopped licking and left his tongue hanging out, resting on my hand. I gave it a gentle pull and said, "Sam, you look silly with your tongue hanging out." He pulled his tongue in, and pushed it into my hand again, so I pulled it again.

"What is this, Sam, some game you want to play with me?" Then Sam raised his head up until his muzzle was in my face. I didn't know what to expect next. Would he lick my face? But he kept his mouth closed and, instead, put one nostril up to my nose. And he gently blew air in my face. Confused, I looked at Buddy. "What's he doing?"

Buddy was a seasoned horseman with Cherokee in his blood. "He's taking in your scent, and offering you his," Buddy replied. "It's a great honor for him to do that—it's a horse's way of saying they trust you enough to want to remember who you are."

Thrilled, I stood very still, and as Sam exhaled, I inhaled; when Sam inhaled, I exhaled. His breath was so sweet. It smelled of fresh grass and sunshine and Sam. *The smell of Sam.* I would never forget it.

Buddy waited patiently until Sam started to walk away from me. "C'mon, Sam, let's go meet your new herd, Prince and Lynn." Buddy led Sam across Wheeler Street and turned him loose with the other horses. Sam sniffed noses with Prince just like he had done with me! When he tried to sniff Lynn, however, Prince got angry and chased him off. The three horses began a bucking romp up and down the steep slopes of the holler that was their pasture. I stood outside the fence and watched them run, wishing with all my heart that Sam was mine.

Chapter Three

Over the winter, Sam grew and filled out. He was not destined to be a large horse. He stood 14.2 hands, or fifty-eight inches high at his withers. Although Sam was not a registered horse, his sire, Three Bars Tonto, had been a registered American Quarter Horse. Three Bars Tonto was a modestly built bay horse, with some Thoroughbred blood in his lineage to add refinement.

Sam's mother, Kickapoo, was a registered American Indian Horse. She came all the way from Arizona. Kickapoo was a tri-colored paint, a lovely bay horse with plenty of white on her body, black points, black mane and tail.

I helped Buddy groom Sam and the other horses every chance I got, so I came to know Sam had a black spot on the inside of his right hind leg, a token from his mother's own tri-colored coat.

Sam had four white feet. His feet were relatively soft and chalky, not flint hard like Prince's black hoofs, so Sam had to wear shoes all the time. He hated getting shoes nailed on, and I hated watching that, too.

Sometimes during those early shoeing sessions, the farrier would wrap a rope all the way around Sam, from his chest to his tail, and then slowly tighten the rope until Sam's legs came together and he fell over, and then the shoes were nailed on while Sam was tied and lying down.

I wept when that happened, and, if horses could cry, I think Sam would have wept, too. I wanted to hold his head in my lap, but the farrier told me to stay away, and Sam was not mine, so I obeyed. But I stood as close as I could and whispered to myself, "Sam, please be brave." In my child's mind, I hoped the air would carry my silent words of encouragement to Sam's ear.

Each time, after the shoeing was over, Sam would get up and come over to me and put his tongue in my hand. I would gently pull his tongue as he licked my hand and we did this over and over and over until he was relaxed and happy again.

In the spring, as Sam was starting his second year, Buddy decided to move all his horses up to Westel Mountain, to a large, rolling pasture that belonged to a friend of his. I was really sad to see the horses go, but Buddy assured me the pasture was full of lush grass and a small stream and that Sam would grow better if he was eating good grass. Westel Mountain was about twenty miles away and, at thirteen, I was much too young to drive legally, even if Mom had been willing to let me use the family car.

I watched as Sam stepped obediently into the horse trailer. I watched as the trailer slowly rolled up Wheeler Street, around the curve, until it was out of sight. Then I went into my room, closed the door, and wept. I knew that was selfish of me, and wrong. Sam was not my horse. But he and I shared breath often, and we played his tongue game, and we had lots of fun together, so it was almost like he was my own horse. And I was going to miss him.

Chapter Four

Springtime in East Tennessee is a glorious event. The crocuses come first, with white and lavender buds pushing through the brown earth and bursting open their happy faces toward the sun. Next come bright clumps of yellow daffodils that seem to spring up overnight and clap their green-leaf-hands in the breeze. On the hillsides, in the woods, white dogwoods frame the pink of blossoming redbud trees, and the entire region springs to life with an avian orchestra playing God's birdsong symphony. The brassy squawks of jays. The lyrical songs of robins and cardinals. The arias of the chickadees and titmice. Glorious.

Unexpectedly, one Saturday afternoon, Buddy again pulled in our driveway with the old red-and-white horse trailer. He was driving fast and jerked to a stop, throwing the truck into park and causing both truck and trailer to rock from the sudden stop. As I went outside to investigate, another truck cut quickly off Wheeler Street and into our driveway, and it, too, slammed to a stop.

The vet's truck.

Even before Buddy opened the back of the trailer, somehow I knew Sam was inside. My heart stopped.

"Some young boys were up on the mountain hunting deer with .22 rifles," Buddy explained as he pulled the trailer door open while the vet got his instruments out. "They didn't find any deer, so they emptied their guns in the only large animal they could find."

"Don't they know the difference between a deer and a horse?" the vet grumbled, tossing surgical instruments into a bucket of sterilizing fluid.

"They didn't know enough to use a .30-30 instead of a .22," Buddy scoffed. He was in the trailer, at Sam's head, slowly steadying the colt as he started to back out of the trailer.

"Well, that probably saved your horse's life," the vet replied. "Let's get him out here and take a look."

I stood off to one side, out of the way, as Sam backed off with unsteady feet. He looked sick and forlorn. His head was low and his eyes were half-closed, and it seemed like every step was a challenge for him to take. Quickly, I scanned his body, expecting to see gaping holes, torn flesh, and rivers of blood pouring out of sweet, gentle Sam.

I was surprised at how little blood there was. All I could see was one small spot near his right elbow. The vet was quick to spy it, too, as he placed his stethoscope just behind Sam's elbow. He listened while he examined the bullet hole, then stood up with a small smile on his face. "Too low to hit his heart."

Mine began to beat again. Rapidly. Maybe he would live!

The vet walked around to Sam's left side. "That shot went clean through! Lucky for you, Buddy; this colt's only two, so he's still narrow in the chest and that bullet didn't hit anything vital."

My heart began to sing! Maybe he was okay!

Then Sam coughed, and it sounded all gurgly and awful. His head hung lower from the effort as he coughed again. The vet kept examining him. "There's something else here, somewhere," he said. He put his stethoscope low on Sam's shoulder, and I wondered why. He'd already said Sam's heart was undamaged, so what was wrong?

The vet knelt down in front of Sam and carefully examined his chest. There, on the left chest muscle, was a small hole with a trickle of blood seeping out.

"They took another shot from the front, Buddy," the vet said. The tone of his voice froze my soul. Buddy looked at the vet, and the two men spoke without saying a word. Frantic, I looked from the vet to Buddy and back again. My mind screamed, "No! No! *NOOOO!*"

The vet's voice seemed far away as he said, "They hit his left lung, Buddy, and he's bleeding internally. That's what's causing the cough."

His voice became a blur as my mind stopped working and I began to pray, *"No! God, please! NO!"*

"Can you do anything?" Buddy asked.

"No. There's no way to take the bullet out. It's possible the lung will collapse, and if that happens . . ."

I watched, horrified, as Buddy nodded to the vet.

"Okay."

Crying openly now, I silently pleaded with God. "Please keep Sam alive—I'll do anything you ask, God! *Anything!*" I'd been regularly attending the local United Methodist Church every Sunday for all of my thirteen years. I figured surely God could do this one tiny favor for me. After all, it wasn't just *any* horse, it was *SAM!*

As the vet stood up and started looking for the right size syringe, I ran up and wrapped my arms around Sam's neck, turning pleading eyes to Buddy.

"No! No, please, Buddy, NO! Please don't! I'll help! I'll do whatever I can, just please give Sam a chance!"

Buddy stood silently for what seemed like forever. He had held great hopes for this colt. He had planned to raise Sam, train him to be a saddle mount, and then sell him to make some much-needed money. Buddy's eldest son needed to have a surgery performed, and the money from Sam was going to help pay for that surgery. Buddy needed Sam. And he needed him alive.

"Doc . . ."

The vet turned and looked at Buddy. He surely saw a pitiful sight. One overworked man who didn't have surplus money for horse injuries and protracted healings and vet bills. One smallish, wounded horse who would die anyway as soon as that lung collapsed. And one young neighbor girl, weeping openly, holding onto the scrawny colt as though her very life depended on him living.

The vet scratched his head and sighed. "Buddy, the next seven days are critical. You'll have to keep this horse on his feet, and moving, nearly 24/7, to make sure the blood keeps flowing through that lung and infection doesn't set it. Even then, you may get infection, or the lung could collapse. Either way, the horse dies a painful death."

I kept my grip on Sam and prayed harder. *Please, God! Please!* "I'll walk him, Buddy! Day and night, I promise! I will! He'll get better, I know he will! We just have to give him that chance!"

Buddy slowly stroked Sam's neck. "Doc, I don't want him to suffer, but I need to try. I really need this horse to live, so I can sell him."

The vet knew about Buddy's son. Everyone who knew the family knew about Buddy's son. With a resigned nod, the vet began to put his equipment back into his truck.

Buddy handed me Sam's lead rope and headed toward the vet, pulling his wallet out as he walked. "Doc, I want to pay you for coming out today."

"I didn't do anything, Buddy, and that colt's most likely going to die, anyway. No charge."

The next seven days were exhausting, yet exhilarating, too. The first two days, Saturday and Sunday, Sam and I spent hour after hour together, slowly walking a few steps, then stopping to rest. We walked in his holler, and the hills were very steep, so we took it really slow. Every hour, I would offer him a little water out of a bright red bucket. Sometimes he would drink, sometimes not.

Sam seemed to perk up whenever he heard a bird singing nearby, so, when the birds were silent, I sang softly to him. The only words I knew from memory were some of the old hymns from the Cokesbury hymnal, so I serenaded Sam with songs like "Amazing Grace" and "His Eye is on the Sparrow." When I'd gone through all the regular hymns I knew, I sang Christmas carols to Sam—"Joy to the World!" and "Angels We Have Heard on High" and, unlike the boys in my Sunday School class, Sam never snickered when I got off-key on all the "Glorias" in that song. My mom and both my sisters were blessed with wonderful soprano voices. I, on the other hand, had little vocal talent, and much preferred to play the piano than sing.

But Sam seemed to enjoy my singing, and as the hours went by, his cough-accompaniment grew quieter. Whenever we stopped so Sam could rest, I would gently stroke his neck and quietly have a three-way conversation with me and Sam and God.

"Sam, God's here with us, you know that, don't you?" Sam's eyes would sometimes be closed. He was fighting to live, and it was a tiring battle. But I knew he was listening, because his ears would always follow my voice.

"God, this is Sam. He's my wonderful friend, and I'm so grateful You blessed me with getting to pretend Sam is my very own. Some really dumb boys shot Sam, and now we need Your help. The vet says Sam's lung is in big trouble. But you've healed folks forever—the Bible teaches all about Your ability to heal! You've made really old ladies have babies. You made the Red Sea part so thousands of people could walk on dry land. You've made a few loaves of bread and a couple of fish feed thousands of folks, and there were even a bunch of baskets of leftovers! So Sam and I *know* You can patch up his lung. And Sam and I are grateful to You for being such a good God that you would fix him up like new. Please. In Jesus' name. Amen."

On Monday, when I had to go back to school, some of Buddy's family took over walking Sam until I got home in the afternoon. My mother never said a word as I quickly changed clothes and ran across Wheeler Street to resume walking Sam. Sometimes, when we walked in view of my house, I thought I caught a glimpse of my mother watching us from a window, but I never took my eyes off Sam long enough to be certain.

On the seventh day, the vet returned.

Chapter Five

"I never thought he'd make it this far," Doc said, shaking his head in disbelief. Sam stood quietly as the vet examined the wounds on his sides and chest and listened to his heart and lungs.

Buddy stood nearby, lounging on the bumper of his pickup with his arms folded across his chest. "Neither did I." He nodded his head toward Sam as he spoke, a slow smile spreading across his face. "I believe more than a few prayers and a least a hundred miles might've helped a bit."

The vet glanced up from Sam's chest and noticed me holding Sam's lead rope. "Had a bit of help walking him, did ya?"

"Couldn't keep her away." Both men chuckled.

I should have been embarrassed, I know. But I didn't care if they were teasing me. Sam was getting better! That's all that mattered.

The vet stood up and stuffed his stethoscope in his pocket. He looked down at me with kind eyes. "You've done a fine job, young lady. His lung isn't 100% yet, but the likelihood of it collapsing on him now is slim." He turned to Buddy.

"All three wounds are healing up fairly well, all things considered." Doc paused, and looked at me, as if to include me the adults' conversation. "He'll carry that slug in his left lung for the rest of his life, you know. Let's just hope it doesn't shift or move."

My feet hardly touched the ground as I led Sam away from the vet to let him nibble on a nearby patch of grass. I was silent on the outside, but inside, I was talking a mile a minute.

"ThankyouthankyouTHANK YOU, GOD! I *knew* You'd take care of Sam! See, Sam, didn't I tell you? God loves you as much as I do, and He'll always take good care of you! Yippee! You're going to *live*!

Sam snorted softly and continued munching lespedeza, a small, tender plant of the sweet pea family, with tiny, yellow blossoms—his favorite legume and one of Sam's favorite treats.

Even though Sam no longer needed constant walking, I continued spending as much time as possible with him. Buddy didn't mind me taking Sam out of the field for short strolls, and soon the two of us spent every afternoon exploring the neighboring pastures. Sam followed along on his lead rope like an oversized retriever, placid and content to be roaming about, exploring new places and getting lots of attention.

I learned where all his favorite itchy places were, too. He loved to be scratched right behind both elbows as the bullet wounds healed. Even after the scabs fell away, he always enjoyed a good rub in those spots. His chest was another favorite. As the summer progressed and the flies got worse, he would lean up against me, asking in his horsey way for me to scratch his belly. Sometimes the flies were so bad my hand came away with spots of blood on it where the flies had bitten fiercely. I would rub as gently as I could, and Sam would stretch his neck out, groaning in satisfaction as the pesky flies flew off his belly. If the flies tried to land on me, I'd move to where Sam's lengthening tail could swipe them off of me with a "swoosh." The ends of his tail stung red streaks on my legs, but I knew Sam wasn't trying to hurt me and I was glad to have his help keeping the flies off. Sam was so quiet-natured that whenever a large horsefly landed on him he would stand very still and let me smack it into a gushy pile on the dirt. Then I'd dig my heel into the fly to make certain it was dead.

I turned fourteen that spring and life was so good! While I didn't own Sam, I got to care for him like he was my own, and that was the next best thing. He wasn't old enough to ride yet, but I didn't care. Just spending time with him was enough.

By June, Sam was completely healed up. Buddy began putting a saddle and bridle on Sam. Sam didn't like the large curb bit or the heavy western saddle. At only twenty-six months old, he was still a very young horse, and sometimes he got off balance when Buddy would stand in the stirrup. Occasionally, Sam got so off-balance he fell, and then he and Buddy would roll down the steep hillside of the holler. I didn't like watching these training sessions, but I always visited Sam once they were over. We would play Sam's pull-the-tongue game and I would tell Sam what a good boy he was to try so hard even though he was still a baby. It never occurred to me that Buddy might have been hurt whenever Sam fell. I only thought of Sam.

Chapter Six

July was hot and sticky. I spent every moment I could with Sam, shooing flies off his belly and brushing him all over until his coat gleamed deep brick red and shiny white under the burning summer sun. The last Saturday of July, mid-morning, Buddy came and talked with me while I brushed Sam.

"Esther, I've made a decision and I wanted to tell you first." The tone of his voice made me stop brushing and look him in the eye.

"I've decided to sell Sam."

I felt the earth tremble and I knew it was my knees. "Do not faint! Keep breathing!" I told myself. Despite the temperature and sunny skies, I was suddenly chilled and shivering.

"I wanted to tell you first, in case there's any way you could buy him."

I couldn't speak. I was fourteen years old. I had no money. I had no job. My mother made a pauper's salary as a schoolteacher, and she still had me and my middle sister, Janie, at home. My elder sister, Frankie, had married and moved away one week after she graduated high school. She was eighteen and couldn't wait to leave our small town for the big city of Memphis, Tennessee.

We never went hungry, but we were so poor my mother would buy the out-of-date bologna at the grocery store and then fry it until the white, sticky film that covered its oldness became a burnt crust. Fried old bologna and grisly Salisbury steak frozen dinners were weekly staples at my house. That and pinto beans. I hate pinto beans. They feel like chalk against my teeth. And the brown liquid everyone else sopped up with cornbread looked like mud soup to me. But I always looked forward to pinto bean night, because, instead of chalky beans in mud, I filled a big soup bowl full of cornbread and drowned it in sweet milk and clover honey from Grandpa's bees.

Buddy knew there was absolutely no way I could ever buy Sam.

"I've had an offer on him—someone wants to buy him and try to turn him into a racking horse."

Sam? I was an obedient child and didn't voice my incredulity at the thought. Sam was bred to be a trail horse or a cow horse. He didn't *rack*! He hated to trot and I rarely ever saw him gallop. He was sweet, steady Sam. He liked to walk. His favorite gait, though, was "nap." Preferably in a cool, shady spot.

I clenched Sam's brush in my hands and forced myself not to cry.

"How much?" My voice sounded small and insignificant.

"One twenty-five."

My heart sank. One hundred and twenty-five dollars was not a bad price for a horse like Sam in those days; I knew that. It was reasonable and fair—and way out of my reach.

"When?" My fingers dug harder into the brush, but I didn't feel the boar bristles poking into my palm.

"End of the month." The three of us stood silently for a bit. Sam stood "hip shot," his weight off-center so one rear hoof was curled onto its toe. He lazily swished his tail at the flies, completely oblivious to the impending, unstoppable disaster that was less than a week away. Finally, Buddy spoke, his voice quiet and tired.

"I'm sorry, Esther."

I put Sam's brush away and handed his lead rope to Buddy. I crossed Wheeler Street with a broken heart. By the time I walked in my front door, I could not stop the tears.

As a child, I was a silent crier. I learned as a toddler that voiced crying only lead to more lashes with my paternal dna's belt. As the youngest, I never felt the buckle end, but the holey end was bad enough.

She never said for sure, but I think my big sister got both ends. I don't know about my middle sister. The holey end made the backs of my legs turn bright red, and my skin stung just like it did the time I accidentally opened the wrong mailbox—an old abandoned one—and a swarm of angry red wasps attacked my legs for so rudely opening their nest's front door. Whippings with the belt felt just like that. So you learned to let the tears flow without making a sound. I was an expert at silent grief.

Still, somehow that day my mother knew I was weeping, and she asked me what was wrong. Hadn't Sam just survived two gunshot wounds not weeks before? What had happened now?

"Buddy is selling Sam."

My mother is a small woman, with black hair, olive skin, and dark brown doe-like eyes. She was born of a long line of Scots, surname Roberts of Clan Donnachaidh on her mother's side, and she said Grandpa's family, Crowder, was of "black Dutch" ancestry, hence the smallish frame and typically dark features that were common amongst my Crowder kin. My own strawberry blonde hair, pale skin, and sapphire blue eyes were either a throwback to my maternal grandmother's old Scottish bloodlines, or inherited from my paternal dna. I claimed my Scottish blood and ignored the other side of my family tree, just as they apparently ignored me and my sisters.

I do not know what went through my mother's mind that day as she stood there and watched her youngest daughter weeping over an impossible dream.

Perhaps she recalled the night when she, Janie and I wanted to go eat supper at the new Long John Silver's that had recently come to our county. Dining out was a rare treat for us. But Gretchen decided we would somehow find the money to go eat fish 'n more. She had a few dollars in her purse—the black purse with its two large chambers and zippered compartment in the center that she never zipped because it was too full of her overly organized, never spontaneous life. We regularly teased her about how her purse had a place for everything and everything in its place, so she could literally find her lipstick while driving down Wheeler Street at what seemed to be breakneck speed without ever taking her eyes off the road. But she emptied the black purse and there were not enough coins in the bottom to buy three fish 'n more dinners. So the three of us went to the car and started searching between the seats, under the floor mats, in the glove compartment. We found pennies sticky with un-recognizable children's shoe goo. There were nickels and dimes, too, and even the rare quarter. By suppertime, we had scavenged enough money to make the merry drive to Long

John Silver's for three fish dinners and three small drinks. It was one of the finest dining experiences I've ever had.

Maybe my mother thought of all the childhood wishes that never came true. "Dear Santa, please bring me a pony. Any color is fine. Thank You." "Mommie, can I ask the Easter Bunny to bring me a pony, please? I'd much rather have a pony than an Easter basket."

She was not overly affectionate with us when we were children. Chronic exhaustion can do that to a parent. I have no fond memories of bedtime stories or afternoons of cookie baking. The closest we ever came to "family time" was late on Friday or Saturday nights when Mother would make homemade waffles and we would sit around the kitchen table, stuffing syrup-soaked waffles into our mouths, happily oblivious to the harsher realities of life. When I received the occasional hug from my mother, I remember feeling warm skin and smelling Jergen's lotion. There was always a bottle of Jergens on my mother's dresser.

But there was no hug today. This dreadful day of bleakest news. Sam was being sold. My mother kept her distance. I continued to stand in front of her and weep silently, too devastated to go to my room. With the faith known only to desperate hearts, I knew I had to try.

"Please, Mama. Isn't there any way? Please?"

I didn't look up at what I knew would be a weary, overburdened face. I knew I was asking for the impossible. I knew I was asking for a miracle. I knew I had to keep asking.

"Please, Mama. He's only one hundred twenty-five dollars. I'll figure out a way to pay you back." It never occurred to me she didn't have one hundred twenty-five dollars. I had no idea.

My mother sighed. "I don't even have twenty-five dollars, Esther. Not for a horse. And besides, we have no place for a horse. This place is only two acres. There's no fence, no barn, nothing. We can't afford the food, the hay, the vet bills. It's just impossible."

"But I could get a job to pay for his food and hay."

"You're only fourteen!"

"But you could sign papers to let me work, couldn't you?"

"That's not the point, Esther. I simply do not have the money. We are not buying a horse!"

"But he's only one hundred and twenty-five dollars, Mama. That's cheap for a horse!"

"The only money I have is two college savings bonds for you! How are you supposed to get an education?"

"I make nearly straight A's, Mom. I'll scholarship my way through school, I promise. How much are the college bonds worth?"

Mother sighed. "A hundred and twenty-five dollars."

I was elated. "That's perfect! If you'll cash out the bonds and buy Sam, and sign papers to let me get a job, I *promise* I'll pay for all his food and stuff and I'll pay you back for him as soon as I can and I'll make good grades all through high school and get a scholarship to college, Mom. I swear I will!"

The glimmer of hope I had momentarily felt was crushed when I saw her jaw set. I knew what that meant. It was utterly ridiculous to even consider the possibility, and both of us knew it. I thought of how empty my fingertips would feel when they could no longer work the tangles out of his mane and tail. I recalled his scent and knew I would never forget the smell of Sam. I remembered the countless hours Sam and I had spent together. I knew every inch of his body. I knew every expression in his eye. I knew Sam right down to the depths of his soul. He wasn't just *a* horse. He was *my* horse.

"Please, Mama. It's not just any horse. It's *Sam*."

You know how when parents sometimes close their eyes and let out their breath in an exasperated huff and then open their eyes and glare at you? It's the universal signal that a child has pushed too far and parental love is battling with the desire to scream bloody murder at the child. Or worse. That was my mother's response.

She silently glared at me for what seemed like forever. I'd never felt such intense scrutiny from another human being in my life. Either she was trying to figure out how to exorcise the equine madness out of her youngest daughter, or wondering just how much mettle a fourteen-year-old girl might have. I can't say exactly what went through her mind that day, but I will never forget her next words.

"Okay," she relented, using her strongest "mom" voice to add weight to her words. "Here's the deal: I'll cash out your college bonds and buy Sam for you. But you will have to get a job and pay all of his expenses. And *you* will have to take care of him all by yourself—I'm not going to help, do you understand? And I expect you to pay your own way through college, young lady."

Through a bursting rainbow of joy, I remember squealing, hugging her, and promising with all my heart to meet her terms.

Chapter Seven

The deal was made on July 31st in our driveway, on the trunk of a faded red Chevrolet Impala Buddy drove. My mother gave Buddy every red cent she had scraped together for my college education, and Buddy gave my mother a check-sized generic receipt. He had my mother fill out the receipt in her schoolteacher's cursive writing. Then he scrawled his signature on the bottom line. As he handed the slip of onion-skin-thin paper back to my mother, I peered over her elbow and saw the only line on the receipt that mattered to me: "*for:* Sam."

Buddy folded the bills and tucked them into his pocket. My mother made a sun visor of one hand and looked across the road at my future education-turned-equine, who stood dozing in the midmorning sun, totally oblivious to the monumental change in his life that had just occurred. I hugged my mother and then wrapped my arms around myself, willing myself to stand still and not jump up and down with sheer delight.

I had a horse! A real, live, breathing horse—*of my very own*! No one could take him away. No one could sell him.

Sam would be mine. *Forever.* I gazed at my sleeping Sam—*my* Sam!

I was naively oblivious to the fact that, while I now owned a horse, that was *all* I owned. One horse. No saddle. No bridle. I didn't even own a brush for Sam! Buddy loaned me a halter and lead rope. Otherwise, I would have had nothing with which to lead Sam around.

"You can keep Sam where he is until you get a fence put up," Buddy offered. "All I ask is you pay for his feed and upkeep while he's still on my place." Buddy was a very kind, fair man.

During my youngest years, Grandpa kept a few cows for beef. Mostly "black baldies," typically black-bodied animals with a white face and chest. Black baldies are a sweet, calm cross of Angus and Hereford that gain weight well but are not as expensive as pure Angus. I do recall he had one white cow, because I watched her give birth in Grandpa's pasture one spring. But the majority of the herd was black baldies and there was one particular cow Grandpa never slaughtered. She was our "riding cow" when I was very young. We grandkids named her "Tammy," and Grandpa would stack us up in a row on her back and let us sit there while Tammy continued grazing, unperturbed.

When he and Grandma sold their little farm and moved to a subdivision, Grandpa had given me the old red-handled currycomb we had used to brush Tammy. So I had Sam and a currycomb. (Tammy, by the way, never did get slaughtered. By the time Grandpa sold the farm, and the cows, Tammy was too old to be good for meat, so the man who bought her just turned her out in a field with some other cows, and she enjoyed a worry-free retirement.)

Some of my mother's friends owned a "mom and pop" fast food restaurant in town, and arrangements were made for me to work there after school and on Saturdays. I washed dishes, swept the floors, and waited on customers. I made one dollar an hour and prioritized my spending by what Sam needed most.

With my first paycheck, my mother drove me to the local farmer's co-op store and I bought Sam some feed, a soft brush, and one small brass swivel snap.

My mother and both my sisters were gifted seamstresses. I never could do much sewing myself, other than taking cheap cotton print fabric and making plain-pocket curtains you scrunch onto those cheap little gold rods, or pillows to match out of the scraps. My mother could make full-length, lined draperies with pleater tape. She could make really pretty Easter dresses, too. I remember watching my mother carefully lay out the pattern pieces on the fabric. She bought just barely enough yardage to make all the pattern pieces fit, and she knew how to set the pattern to take even less yardage than the pattern packet called for. Often, she took apart an old dress she had made and redesigned it and cut it down to fit me or one of my sisters. I always wanted a store-bought dress instead of a re-worked hand-me-down from a previous Easter. Funny how that works; these days I would love to have my own private seamstress.

But the point is this: I didn't have enough money to buy Sam a halter and lead rope on that first trip to the co-op, so I took some thick embroidery trim and some plastic rings from my mother's vast collection of sewing notions and I clumsily sewed Sam a halter, breaking more than one of my mother's best Singer machine needles in the process. I got a spool of twine and macraméd Sam a lead-rope, attaching the brass swivel snap I had bought at the co-op.

Sam got spooked one afternoon while he was wearing his homemade embroidered halter, when the plastic rings broke with a "pop." It sounded like small gunfire right around Sam's head. He didn't bolt, but just stood there with a wild look in his eye and pathetic strips of embroidery trim hanging off his ears and nose. On my next trip to the co-op, I had enough money for a brand new nylon halter for Sam. The halters came in blue, green, and red. Given Sam's brick-red face, I chose green. That halter never broke but worked faithfully for years, until much later, when I could finally afford a soft, leather halter for Sam, complete with an engraved brass nameplate on the cheek strap.

My mother helped me chop down mimosa trees in our yard to cut up and make into fence posts. She did most of the chopping, truth be told, but I did swing the ax a few times and make an effort to help. I'm not sure if she realized mimosa wood is soft, thus relatively easy to cut down with an old, dull ax, or if the mimosas were the only trees she was willing to sacrifice for a horse fence. My mother has always loved nature, and more than once she argued with the local power company when they would come along the edge of Wheeler Street with their oversized chain saws to clear branches out of the power lines before winter began. She watched every limb fall with a horrified expression on her face, as though the utility men were cutting off her own fingers and toes.

But, for whatever reason, the first fence posts for Sam were made of mimosa wood. The posts were not straight because mimosas have bends and branches along the trunk. Some were five inches in diameter. Some were two inches in diameter. We dug holes in the scrabbly earth and used a broom handle to tamp the dusty soil around each mimosa post. Our house sat on a grand total of two acres, so Mother was only willing to let Sam have about one-half an acre for

My Friend Sam

his home. I would have happily let him live in the basement, but my mother and sisters didn't favor that notion.

Before too many weekends, all the posts were in the ground. With my next trip to the co-op, I bought one spool of thin, plain wire, two bags of plastic insulators, a small "shock box" and battery, and a red plastic insulated handle. Fancy, woven-wire horse fencing was too expensive. Sam would live in an electric fence.

My mother and I nailed the plastic insulators to the mimosa fence posts. Some of the posts wobbled under the hammer strikes. Some of the nails didn't get hammered in all the way. For those nails, we hammered until they stopped going into the post, and then hammered the nail head sideways so it wouldn't stick out and snag our clothes. We made a rough, wooden box to house the shock box and battery, and nailed the box to a gnarly pine tree that was one of the "corners" of the pasture. I didn't have enough money to buy creosote corner posts and brace wire, so, instead of a carefully measured square paddock, Sam's fence line was determined by where the largest living trees were, and they became the corners and support for the fence. Sam's first fence had six "corners" and defied geometry.

All in all, it was a pathetic, homespun excuse for a "fence," but I didn't see all the weaknesses at the time. As I twisted the wire through the red plastic handle, and my mother wired the shock box to the battery terminals, the steady, audible "tick" of the shock box told me the fence was hot, and Sam could finally come home to live with me.

In my mind, moving Sam to his new home was a huge celebration, just like when those Thoroughbreds arrive at Churchill Downs and walk regally down the ramps of those big eighteen-wheeler horse hauling vans, with their colorful traveling sheets on and their porcelain legs carefully wrapped with thick cotton bandages to protect them from injury. Their heads are up and their eyes are keen and the wind whips their manes and tails until they look like some larger-than-life god of the wind as they prance around and nearly pull their handlers off the ground.

In reality, I put Sam's new green halter on him, clipped his macramé lead to the ring under his chin, and walked him across Wheeler Street, down my driveway, around behind the house, and into his new "pasture." He had no traveling sheet, nor cotton shipping bandages. His mane was not whipped by the wind, nor did he raise his head with brilliant defiance. He simply walked along beside me, clip-clopping along with his head down by my shoulder. Sam liked to walk where we could see eye-to-eye. And that suited me just fine.

To my knowledge, Sam only hit the electric fence once, and he wasn't trying to run away then. He was stretching under the fence to get some elusive blades of grass, and the fence came into contact with his outstretched neck. He backed up quickly and looked at me with surprise in his eyes. He never tested the fence again. Smart Sam.

I'm not sure when, or how, my mother told my grandfather that she had bought a horse. I can only imagine the uproar, because Grandpa was a frugal man. He had learned to be careful with every penny out of necessity. He had assumed responsibility for his entire family at age fourteen. He had lost the sight in one eye because of a farming accident sometime in his youth, yet he had worked his family farm despite his disability and provided food, clothing, and a modest education for all of his siblings. If he hadn't shown such great aptitude for mathematics and the sciences in high school, grandpa probably would have died a farmer.

But he had been blessed with a brilliant mind, and his high school teachers realized he had academic potential, despite his many absences during planting and harvest times. His teachers made arrangements for young Tom to become a working student at Tennessee Technological University. It had taken him several years to get through college, but he ended up teaching algebra, calculus, chemistry and physics at more than one high school in East Tennessee. He even worked at Oak Ridge for a while, and invented something new and got it patented.

My grandfather was a brilliant man. And, in his mind, it was utter foolishness for his divorced daughter to invest his granddaughter's college bonds in a horse.

Grandpa, however, was also a pragmatist, so shortly after the fence was up and Sam was home, he arrived at our house one weekend with his pale turquoise Plymouth Fury III and his homemade utility trailer, which was loaded with some concrete block and a whole pile of new lumber, as well as some galvanized tin roofing material. I have no idea how it all came about, but I was grateful—such a load of materials would have cost me a year's worth of weekly paychecks!

My grandfather was the only sane, stable male presence in my youth, and I adored him. I loved his deep voice with the scratchy edge, especially when he got irritated at some minor annoyance and said, "Shuckins." I never heard my grandfather swear, ever. He was a devoted Mason and always wore a coat and tie to church. I loved all his farm animals, from the cows with their warm, rough tongues that wrapped around tiny hands that reached out to pet their slimy noses, to the goldfish Grandpa kept in his stock tank to eat the algae. I learned a great deal just from watching Grandpa. Like how to curry a cow in the direction the hair grows. And how to stay out of pecking range of the rooster.

Grandpa and I played countless checker tournaments and he always let me be red. Sometimes, in the heat of summer, when I was perhaps three years old, Grandpa would scrub out three galvanized tubs and put them under large shade trees in the yard. He would then fill them with cool water. My two sisters and I would then strip down to our "step-ins" (my mother never called underwear "panties") and play in our individual galvanized swimming pools. With only ten inches of water in each thirty-six inch square tub, it was hardly Olympic sized, but we didn't care. Those were our swimming pools, and Grandpa was a genius in our eyes for giving us a cool spot in those days before air conditioning.

My adoration of my grandfather soared when he arrived with the materials to build Sam a barn. I remember every careful step of the process. First, Grandpa put five stakes in the ground, carefully measuring out four corners and pounding the fifth stake in the ground in the middle of the square. Then he took some twine and made a string square, with the stakes as the corners. He also went diagonal across the square, wrapping the twine around the center stake. He took out some gismo from his pocket and measured the angles everywhere. That seemed to take a very long time to me, as he tweaked his stakes a bit here or a tad there until he was satisfied.

Next, we dug a trench in the dirt, following the perimeter string square. Sam wandered up and began munching on the tufts of grass that clung to the clods of dirt we were tossing out of the trench. Grandpa never commented on Sam. At all. Never said he was the most beautiful horse in the universe. Never said he was a smart and good boy. Nothing. He just focused on his project and left Sam alone. Sam seemed content to do the same.

My Friend Sam

We placed the concrete block into the trench, and Grandpa took great pains to make sure the overall surface of the block line was level. The block went all along three sides, and halfway along the fourth. When I asked Grandpa why the block didn't go completely around the edge, he replied, "no need to put block where the doorway will be." So Sam's barn was to be a three and a half-sided run in shed. Fine with me. I was just grateful my beloved pet would have shelter before winter set in.

When it came time to start building the frame, my mother came and helped us. She and I held the two-by-fours together while Grandpa hammered. First a large square of four studs, like a roughhewn, oversized picture frame, then additional two-by-fours about every two feet. Next, Grandpa put a longer two-by-four diagonally from end to end. Then we had to stand that section of framing up and hold it while Grandpa drilled holes and attached it to the concrete blocks. My arms ached from holding the framing in place, but I didn't complain. Sam was getting a barn, and it would be strong enough to withstand any storm!

Once the framing was up all around the three and a half sides, we got a ladder and Grandpa added some framing boards all along the top, so the galvanized tin roofing sheets would have some support.

After all the framing was done, my mother and I carried one-by-sixes from the utility trailer to Grandpa, and he nailed them up to be siding for the barn. Getting the galvanized tin roofing up on top was the hardest part, and we all struggled to get them in place. I didn't realize it at the time, but the ridges had to overlap a certain way to prevent leaks during rain. I am grateful Grandpa knew how to make sure the barn was snug and dry.

As the roofing went on, the interior of the barn became shaded. Dark and cool. It would become one of Sam's very favorite spots, to stand in the doorway of his three-and-a-half-sided shed barn and loaf. He didn't have a door, but that was okay, because I wanted Sam to be able to come and go as he pleased. I hated every minute I had ever been sequestered in my own bedroom, so I wasn't about to lock Sam up.

All in all, it was a fine barn for Sam, and he seemed completely at ease in his small, backyard home.

I bought an old, cast iron bathtub from a neighbor who was kind enough to deliver it, and that became Sam's water trough. I ran a garden hose from the spigot on the back of our house down to the bathtub, so it was easy to fill in warm weather. Sometimes, if I didn't keep the tub completely full of water and it got down to just an inch or so, Sam would be mischievous and pull the plug out with his teeth. More than one afternoon I came home to find a dusty bathtub, a thirsty horse, and the plug somewhere in the field, wherever Sam had dropped it when he tired of nosing it around the dirt.

I bought a large galvanized trashcan to store Sam's feed in. Every two weeks, my mother would drive me to the co-op to buy two more bags of horse feed.

Buddy helped me find a hay supplier and my mother let me store the hay bales on the carport to keep them dry.

I also bought a salt block and put it in Sam's field. At fifty pounds, it was incredibly heavy and difficult to carry, so I set it down and rolled it down the yard and under the fence. There was no money for one of those fancy black plastic salt block holders, and the grass all around the salt block soon dried up and died.

Chapter Eight

Returning to school that autumn was a great celebration for me. I was a freshman in high school, but the only thing that mattered was *I had a horse*! I worked four evenings a week, plus Saturdays, to pay for Sam. Friday nights I didn't work, because I was first chair clarinet in the band and we had football games every Friday.

I've had nightmares all my life, and when I was a small child, I would wake up and toddle to my mother's bed (my parents had twin beds and did not sleep together) and beg her to let me sleep with her, which she always did. Once my parents divorced, the nightmares got so bad that my mother allowed me to move into her bedroom and take up quarters in the other now-vacant twin bed. Her only rule was, "You get one chest of drawers, over here in the corner, and you better never leave a mess anywhere!" So from age seven, I've been disciplined and tidy.

Now, with high school courses, band, a job, and Sam, I was one very busy student. I would hear the other band members laughing together after band practice, planning fun outings or overnight slumber parties. I would hear the other honor students in groups in the hallway, planning meetings or events. I didn't run with the cool kids or the cheerleaders or any other typical high school clique. I was alone, and a loner, incessantly exhausted and often dropping off to sleep in class. But none of it mattered. I had Sam!

I would hear other kids talking about staying out late. I never did. I had to be home to feed Sam his supper.

Other kids would talk about sleeping until noon on the weekend. I never did. I was always up by seven. Sam would be standing at the gate, waiting for his breakfast.

I didn't meet up with friends after school at the local drug store fountain and buy cokes or ice cream sodas or Mayfield's ice cream sandwiches—my favorite. Every penny I earned went to take care of Sam. And that was just fine with me.

On Sunday afternoons, once my homework was finished, I generally had a few hours to spend with Sam. That was heaven. I would put on his green halter and macramé lead rope, and take him out in the yard and let him graze. I had neither saddle nor bridle, and I didn't care. Just *being* with Sam was enough. I brushed his coat until it glistened and there were no more tangles in his mane and tail. Sometimes, I would tie the loose end of the lead rope to the other side of his halter, and climb up and sit on Sam while he ate. Sometimes I would take a book, and read while he wandered around the yard, nibbling on his favorite weeds and grasses. Lespedeza was candy to Sam. He also liked a couple of broad-leafed weeds and dandelion blossoms. I talked to Sam, and sang to Sam, and he seemed to understand every word. He was a grand confidante for a fourteen-year-old girl, being exquisitely good at keeping secrets.

On the coldest days of winter, when Sam's bathtub water trough froze solid, I would take my mother's ax and pound on the ice until it broke into huge chunks. I would fish the slippery ice chunks out and dump them on the ground. Then I took two buckets and made innumerable trips between the outside spigot at the back of our house and Sam's bathtub, sloshing a goodly amount of the contents on my legs and boots as I carried water down to Sam.

My mother gave me an old, threadbare cashmere coat of hers to keep me warm tending Sam during the winter. It was a fine lady's coat in its day, with one large button in the middle of the front lapel. That might have been okay for fine ladies, but that single button didn't keep the coat around my legs very well, and they were always cold and wet from carrying the water buckets down to the bathtub. Still, I was grateful for the warmth of the coat on my shoulders, and it was all for Sam.

Before Sam, I had always looked forward to winter, with its frosty cold air and snow days out of school. Having a horse taught me the harsher aspects of winter life, and I was grateful when the daffodils began peeking through the earth in late February each year.

I kept working, kept playing the clarinet in the band, kept my grades up, and continued to be grateful every day for Sam. I also kept teaching myself piano by ear. My mother was an accomplished piano player, of sorts. She never played Bach or Beethoven. She played hymns from the Cokesbury Hymnal, or wonderful songs like, "Cherry Pink and Apple Blossom White," "Begin the Beguine," "Fascination," and "Sentimental Journey." I had taken piano lessons for a short while during second grade, but, after the divorce, there was no money for private lessons. So I played by ear at home by myself, picking out the right hand part after listening to my mother practice. And my band instructor taught us to read music, so that was helpful. I loved music, melody and rhythm. Life was good.

Then one afternoon, we heard on the news that a tanker truck had wrecked on I-40, and bromine gas was pouring out of the truck and down the mountain. Everyone was warned to stay inside and not breathe the air. I remember how my nose felt acidy and my lungs burned when I went to feed Sam his supper. The air had an orange haze to it, but maybe that was just the sun going down?

Sam ate his evening grain with his usual enthusiasm. He didn't seem stressed at all. So I talked to him and said, "It'll be okay, Sam. God will take care of both of us."

As the evening progressed, however, the newscaster said the bromine spill was worse than originally thought, and that everyone in the area was urged to evacuate. My eldest sister was married and gone by then, but my middle sister still lived at home. She was going to a technical school in Knoxville, though, and needed to get to class the next day. My mother called my grandparents and they debated about what to do. In the end, my mother decided to stay home and trust the heat pump in our home to filter out the bromine gas that night. So, while police cars came down Wheeler Street with their loudspeakers saying, "Evacuate! Evacuate!" we brushed our teeth and put on our nightgowns and went to sleep in our own beds.

The next morning, the radio told us that all local schools were closed because of the bromine gas. Knoxville was unaffected by the gas spill, however, and my sister had to get to class. So she left the house that morning at her usual time. Thirty minutes later, she returned, followed by an army jeep carrying four National Guardsmen. The men were in army fatigues and they looked very serious as they followed my sister up the driveway. My mother met them at our front door.

"Ma'am, y'all need to evacuate, ma'am." Polite. The military personnel are always polite.

"Mama, I was just trying to get to school, Mama, but they've got jeeps at all the main roads out of town, and when I tried to leave, they made me turn around and they followed me home. How am I going to get to school now, Mama?" My sister had always hated school and had never wanted to attend college, so she chose this technical school to get trained as an electronics technician. She was paying for it herself, and missing a day of classes was an expensive nuisance.

"Sir," my mother, too, was always polite, "surely it's okay for us to stay here. We're staying indoors, and we have a heat pump. My daughter needs to get to Knoxville to attend class today."

"She can go to class, Ma'am," the nice young Guardsman assured my mother. "In fact, we insist she leave as soon as possible, along with you and everyone else in the house, as well. The problem is, she can't come back. At least, not until we get the all-clear on this bromine spill."

"And when might that be, may I ask?" My mother's voice was heavy with concern.

"I'm not sure, ma'am. At least one day, maybe two. Maybe even three. It depends on the atmosphere and how rapidly this gas disburses so that it's safe to breathe out here. But all y'all have to leave. Right now. We'll escort you to the edge of town."

I was standing in the background, behind my mother, *willing* those men in army green to leave. Evacuating was unthinkable! We had no truck! We had no trailer! *I will NOT leave Sam*! I silently vowed.

"Can we take T.C., Mama—please?" T.C. was my sister's dog.

"Mama and Daddy don't like pets in the house, but I'm sure they'll understand in this case," my mother assured my sister.

For the first time in my life, I panicked enough to buck authority.

"Mama—we *can't* go! What about *SAM?*" I was quickly getting frantic.

"Who is Sam, Ma'am?" the polite Guardsman asked.

"My daughter's horse," my mother replied. Then she looked at me and my heart sank.

"Esther, we have to. These men won't let us stay, now that they know we're here."

"That's right, Ma'am. We have to escort you, and we need to leave as soon as possible."

"I *won't* leave Sam! *I won't leave Sam!*" I could hear hysteria rising in my voice, as tears began to trickle down my cheeks.

The nice young Guardsman tried to reason with me, to no avail. "He should be all right. Just give him plenty of hay and water and he'll be okay."

"Then if it's okay for *him* to stay, it's okay for *me* to stay, and I'm *not leaving my horse behind*!" A horrible battle was going on inside me as a terrified teenager and an enraged equestrienne tried to make The United States Army understand.

The nice young Guardsman looked at my mother with a resigned eye. "Ma'am, if you'll gather what you need, quickly, we'll escort you to the edge of town."

My sister was already packing, gathering T.C.'s collar and leash. My mother turned to me and spoke as firmly as she could. "I'll pack your clothes. You go and tend your horse."

"But *Mama!*" I was hysterical.

"Go. Now."

"NOOO!" I screamed, as I headed to the carport to get Sam's feed and a whole bale of hay. "I WILL NOT LEAVE SAM! I WILL NOT LEAVE HIM!"

I fed my beloved horse through a fog of tears and an orange haze. Breathing was nearly impossible, and Sam had his head down. "Oh, Sam! I don't know what to do! I'm not old enough to drive and I don't have a truck and trailer! I'm SOOO sorry, Sam! But I *swear* to you, that one day, as soon as I can, I'll buy a truck, and a trailer, and I will *never* leave you behind again! EVER!"

I stayed with Sam until my mother came to the fence. "C'mon, Esther. We have to go." I was praying a fervent prayer to protect Sam, and never took my eyes off Sam as I left his fence. My mother took my arm by the wrist, tightly, and I never felt a thing. As we got near the cars, and the jeep full of Guardsmen, I knew such a feeling of utter helplessness, total powerlessness, that I simply had to strike out.

"I *hate* you! All of you! If it's safe for Sam, it's safe for me! And if it's not safe for Sam, I don't want to leave him! I *hate* you! I HATE YOU!"

My mother forced me into her car as I screamed, my voice raw and the tears streaming nonstop down my face. "I HATE YOU!"

My sister's car led the way, my mother in the middle, and the jeep full of nice young Guardsmen stayed right behind us until we were at the edge of town.

We were gone for two days. And for two days, I did not sleep. For two days, I did not eat. For two days, I did not speak. I stood at one window in my grandparents' home, the window that faced the way home, and I prayed for Sam's forgiveness. I had done the unthinkable.

I had abandoned my horse.

Chapter Nine

All I remember about the drive back home is that my mother drove too slowly. I have no idea if she hit eighty miles per hour, and it didn't matter—it was too slow. I had the car door open before she ever put the vehicle in park, and ran down the carport steps to Sam's pasture. Sam was not standing anywhere.

"Oh, God, NO!" I ducked under the electric fence and searched frantically for any trace of a hole in the fence. The fence was secure, so he hadn't gotten loose. I closed my eyes and then opened them again, steeling myself as I looked all around for Sam's sorrel and white coat, lying on the ground.

But there was nothing. No sign. No hair. No trace.

"Sam!" I called, terrified of the worst. "SAM!"

Under now-clear, blue skies, a familiar brick-red face peered around the edge of the barn. I sat down on the ground as my legs gave way with relief. Sam slowly ambled up to me and put his nose near my head, fluffing my hair with his breath. I reached up and hugged his neck.

"Sam! Oh, Thank You, God!"

I stood up and checked Sam all over for any signs of sickness or anything. I had no idea what bromine gas might do, but I knew Sam's left lung carried a bullet. But he seemed totally fine, and his breathing was clear.

My heart grew dark when I recalled my leaving, two days before. "Sam, I *swear* to you by all that is holy, someday I'll have a truck and a horse trailer and I will *never* leave you again. I *swear!*"

So I continued to work, and I put any extra money in an envelope in my top dresser drawer. When my eldest sister had married and left home, her bedroom had become available, so I now enjoyed a corner bedroom with two windows. Best of all, the back window faced Sam's pasture, so I could just look out my bedroom window and see Sam out there.

By the start of my junior year of high school, in two short years, the mimosa posts had rotted and Sam's fence began to fall. I was working two jobs now, and driving, too. My mother had taken me to the driver's license station immediately after my sixteenth birthday. I took the written test, the eye test, and the driving test. She had me drive her back to her school and, when we got there, she handed me a spare set of car keys and said, "I don't ever want to chauffer another child again." So, with that, I drove her to school and pretty much had use of the car whenever I needed it.

The local veterinarian offered me a job to be his assistant. That paid much better than washing dishes at a hamburger joint, and I got to do all sorts of interesting stuff, from helping dry kittens and put them in an incubator after a cesarean section, to hacking open a frozen cow carcass with an ax in the middle of winter to see why she died. Frozen was better than hot summer post mortems, however. Rigor mortis stinks in July.

I thought I wanted to become a veterinarian at that time. My vocational choice changed over time, though. I still remember the times people would bring in litters of perfect puppies or kittens, their only flaw being unwanted. I realize they could have been thrown in dumpsters, drown or stoned to death, and that euthanasia was the only "humane" way. But to this day I am haunted by knowing that my hands held each one of those tiny lives while the vet injected blue fluid into their little veins.

I spoke to them and told them how precious they were as each body went limp in my hands. I asked God to forgive me and all of us humans who so thoughtlessly neglect to spay or neuter animals and then so callously kill their babies. And all for what crime? The "crime" of being unwanted. It was, and is, the most heinous part of veterinary medicine.

I also developed an extreme dislike for people who cut off their dog's ears, all in the name of "fashion." If you could see the pain and confusion a Doberman or Schnauzer puppy goes through as they wake up with ear braces on their ravaged ears, the whole world would outlaw ear trims. Better that it's done under anesthesia and in a sterile environment by a professional veterinarian than by those unlicensed barbarians who cut ears in their garage or breeding shed, but still, it is a wretched practice. That floppy ear is divinely engineered to keep out dust and dirt and muffle loud noises. *Leave it alone.*

So, while I adored drying off preemie kittens and puppies and watching them wriggle to life, or helping some cat with a chart notation of "HBC" (hit by car) regain use of its fractured jaw, in the end, I knew veterinary medicine could never be my lifetime vocation.

My other job was playing piano for a local church on Sundays. Other than Christmas and Easter, that was fairly easy work, and I was grateful for the extra money, especially now that Sam needed a new fence.

Trying to think like Grandpa would, I drew a better, straighter fence line out on paper, and figured up how many new posts I would need, along with how much proper horse fencing. I wanted to give Sam the best fence I could, so I chose seven-inch-diameter creosote posts. For the wire, I selected Red Brand woven wire, four feet high. Woven wire is actually a grid of coated steel strands made in little rectangles, two inches by four inches, small enough that a hoof can't get through, so it is very safe for horses and it also lasts a really long time. For his new fence, Sam would also get a proper galvanized steel gate. No more one-strand electric fence for Sam! It never entered my mind that the fence I was about to build would hold an angry bull!

The co-op delivered the fencing materials, and a young man from my church volunteered to help me build Sam's fence. He had plans to be a minister, and with his handsome face, masculine frame, and rich, baritone voice, he was destined to be a successful one. He had the soft, white hands of a scholar, however, and I'm not sure he'd ever done much manual labor. And, as I said, those seven-inch-diameter posts were—I now know—tremendous overkill for a 14.2 hand, quiet-natured horse who had never broken through a single-strand electric fence!

But this kind young man never complained as he pounded the rock-hard East Tennessee clay with some old posthole diggers. Since Sam was still living inside his old fence, we couldn't reuse the original postholes. So, over the course of one weekend, I and Mr. Minister-to-be dutifully dug somewhere around fifty new holes, set those massive creosote posts in them, and tamped them until they stood upright, tall and proud sentinels to guard against any attempt at escape by my distinctly *un*wild horse. It was extremely hard work, but I didn't mind. It was, after all, for Sam. Mr. Minister-to-be, however, had no vested interest in seeing Sam housed in a safe enclosure. He was simply being kind. And I am forever grateful to him for his kindness.

Rolling out the woven wire was a walk in the park compared to setting those heavy posts, so the rest of the project was completed with relative ease. I remember the happy moment when I unhooked the battery wires for the shock box. I carefully rolled up the electric wire and Sam quickly wandered around to investigate the new fence. I kicked some of the rotten mimosa posts down, watching the ants and termites scramble back under cover as the disintegrated wood gave way. There were a few, fashioned from the thicker sections of trunk, that did not yield to my foot. I left them standing, but by the next summer, every trace of mimosa posts had vanished.

Chapter Ten

Having a horse of my own taught me a great deal about hard work and time management. In retrospect, using my college bonds to buy Sam was, arguably, one of the smartest things my mother could have done to educate her youngest daughter about various aspects of life, including setting priorities and finding adequate substitutes for things that, in the long run, really don't matter very much.

I recall when my classmates were ordering school jackets and senior class rings. Maybe those jackets aren't so much "the thing" these days, but when I was in high school, jackets were really important, and all the kids had them. The jocks put their letters on them. The smart kids put their honors chevrons on them, as did the band kids with their music chevrons. My high school colors were green and gold, and the jackets in the order brochure looked glorious! I had my own honors chevrons and band chevrons tucked safely in a drawer. Probably nobody noticed, but I really wanted a jacket to sew my chevrons onto.

I took the brochure home, but never said a word to my mother about buying a letter jacket. We had no money for such things, and that was okay, because I had Sam. Sometimes, alone in my room, I would open my dresser drawer and lift out my chevrons and make various patterns out of them on the top of my dresser, fingering their looped yarn and imaging me in a beautiful letter jacket, with my chevrons on the shoulders for all the world to see! Then I would tuck the chevrons back amongst my socks and step-ins, and go to bed. The brochure became crinkled with all my wishing, night after night.

We had little money for dry-cleaning, either, and usually the only time those clear plastic bags entered my house was when my mother had one of her Eastern Star gowns cleaned. She was always extremely active in the Eastern Star, and I've enjoyed many a fine covered-dish meal at various Masonic halls across East Tennessee. My mother could not afford babysitters very often, so typically I would travel with her and wait outside in the lobby of the Masonic hall until the meeting was over and then enjoy all sorts of casseroles, sliced ham, rainbows of jello, and a smorgasbord of desserts. Eastern Star ladies are really good cooks. It never occurred to me to wonder why no other children ever attended Eastern Star. The Eastern Star ladies in their elegant evening gowns, and the Masons who attended their meetings in dark suits, white shirts, and ties, were always very nice to me. They offered me fresh lemonade, or sweet iced tea, and made sure I had a full plate, while they complimented my mother on her fine piano playing for that particular meeting. For Eastern Star, my mother always wore her best jewelry and her petticoats made her taffeta gowns go "swish-swoosh" as she walked. She looked as regal as a queen.

So I was surprised one day when my mother brought a dry-cleaning bag into the house, and it did not contain an Eastern Star gown. As she slowly pulled up the plastic, I saw to my amazement and delight, a letter jacket! It was not green and gold, but rather, my high school's old colors of green and white. The knit cuffs were slightly frayed, and when I tried it on, it was at least two sizes too big, but I didn't care. On the back was a fierce-looking tiger head out of white felt! And the shoulders of the sleeves were bare—just *waiting* for chevrons to be sewn on!

"I found it in the school's clothes closet," my mother explained. "It's not new, but it's clean now, and I'll stitch the cuffs so they don't unravel further." My mother was a very proud woman, and she had endured untold scorn, having divorced her philandering, abusive husband and thus dropping several notches in "polite" society's eyes. She had never in her life taken used clothes from a clothes closet, either at school or at church. She made all our clothes, except things like socks and step-ins. As I looked at my not-new letter jacket, I realized what my mother had sacrificed to get it for me. A price far higher than dollars and cents. My mother paid with her pride.

She carefully mended the cuffs, and sewed my honors chevrons on one shoulder and my band chevrons on the other shoulder, and a big white letter "R" on the left front. I wore that jacket with so much pride; it didn't matter if any of the other kids snickered behind my back as they sported their new green and gold jackets around the halls of the high school. My jacket was green and white. Sam was red and white.

At about that same time, orders were being taken for my class's senior rings. Another slick brochure to bring home and so many options to "make your senior ring uniquely yours." White or yellow gold. Stones of every color imaginable. Classic styles. Dainty styles. Put your graduation year on one side, your school initials on the other. Have your name engraved inside. Every option added to the price.

Sam needed hay.

I remember the price of an average senior ring was almost exactly the same amount as the cost of a winter's supply of hay for Sam. It was a no-brainer. I bought hay.

The ordering period for senior rings came and went. A few weeks later, the halls were abuzz with the news that the rings would be delivered very soon. Everyone was eager to get their senior ring. Some wanted to wear their own. Some wanted to wear their beau's, or put it on a chain around their neck. But everyone wanted to show off their new ring the moment they arrived.

The night before senior rings would be distributed, my mother called me into her bedroom. She opened her jewelry box that sat on her dresser. It was antique white with a faded pink satin lining, about the size of a silverware chest.

"I have something for you to wear," she said. And she reached in and lifted out a silver ring. It was shaped like a miniature, classic senior ring. Instead of a stone, it had a solid gold top. On one side, a flying insect was etched into the silver. On the other, the numbers 45.

I took it from her, wondering what it was and why she was giving it to me.

"It's my own senior ring," she explained. I must have looked shocked, because she laughed and said, "es, I *did* graduate high school, young lady." I knew she even had a college degree, so that wasn't what surprised me. Up until that moment, I had never considered that my own parent might have been a young girl once, with her own dreams, her own life and her own senior year. I had only known her as my mother. Now, I had a glimpse of Gretchen, the *girl*.

"Tell me about it, please!" I begged.

"Well, that's a yellow jacket on the side, because I attended Roane County High School. And, back in the war, jewels were really scarce, so nobody had a colored stone on the top of their senior ring. They used this two-tone style, gold on top and silver on bottom."

"How many were in your senior class?"

"About thirty, and all girls." Her mouth drooped like it always did whenever she was tired, or sad. Or both.

"All girls? No boys at all?" What an odd thing, I thought.

"The boys were all gone off to war," she explained. We both stood silently for a time. She seemed lost in her thoughts, and I had absolutely no idea what to say. Finally, she broke out of her musings, and spoke again.

"Try it on, see if it fits."

I slipped on my mother's senior ring, and it fit perfectly. With the loyalty known only to high school seniors and millionaire alumni from SEC colleges, I silently wished it had a tiger on it instead of our rival's yellow jacket. Still, I was grateful to my mother. I would not have a bare hand at school the next day.

It wasn't until many years later that I learned that my mother had graduated Valedictorian of the Roane County High School all-female class of 1945.

Chapter Eleven

I didn't date much at all while in high school. Oh, I had one or two "boyfriends" for short periods of time, but nothing serious. In the first place, my primary focus was Sam. In the second place, I had two older sisters, both of whom were beautiful and charming. In comparison, I felt awkward and shy around boys, and my best guess is the boys in my class found me somewhat goofy and totally unsophisticated. I didn't wear the latest shades of eyeshadow and lipstick. I didn't use makeup at all. I showered and shampooed my long, straight hair every day, but otherwise, I took little notice of my person, and I'm sure I looked every inch a farm girl.

I did attend both my junior and senior proms, in dresses made by my mother and escorted by young men whom I invited. To some, prom night is a festive occasion filled with luxurious dinner, a lively dance party, and then afterparties until sunrise. My experience was more of the sideline variety, but I don't blame the young men. I was hardly captivating company, I am certain. My best prom memory was being driven in a black Chevy SuperSport and enjoying the aggressive purr of the motor as we sped up the highway. A fine machine, indeed.

My grades were high enough at graduation to warrant a class ranking of fourth. The top four students gave speeches at commencement. Being musically inclined, I chose a pop song as the basis of my speech and utilized the lyric as the opening. "People. People who need people are the luckiest people in the world." I don't recall the speech exactly, but I do remember talking about how we students needed the support of our elders and our community in order to succeed, to fulfill our individual and generational destinies, and, hopefully, to have a positive impact on the world. While my English teachers made me and the other three speech-givers practice a time or two, what I recall most is that I practiced my speech with Sam until I felt confident.

Sam was a great audience. Time and again I stood near him or sat on him with my three-by-five notecards, reciting my speech again and again, while he grazed or napped or swished his tail at the occasional springtime fly. The evening of commencement, I don't recall whether I stumbled over the words or if the speech went flawlessly. I do recall a couple of grass stains on my index cards—the result, no doubt, of my equine critic's nibbles at the edges.

At commencement, scholarship awards were announced. Some of my classmates were going away to very prestigious universities. Others were attending college on athletic scholarships. I was absolutely thrilled when my own name was read, citing a full academic scholarship to the local community college. It was the only school to which I had applied. Commuting from home meant Sam and I would not be separated.

I had studied the clarinet since the fifth grade in school band and continued to play the piano by ear. Imagine my delight when, upon registering for college that August, I realized that I could take private piano lessons as a college course! My dream of studying piano could finally come true!

I also became active in the college jazz ensemble, transferring my clarinet knowledge to the saxophone. I was never comfortable playing improvised solos, but I loved being part of a band of musicians, and jazz musicians are the coolest. I'd never before heard of Miles Davis and Herbie Hancock. I learned tunes like, "the 'A' train" and "String of Pearls" and immersed myself in the world of sound.

My piano skills were horrible from a technical standpoint, but my piano teacher was patient and highly skilled, and she helped me work to develop correct fingering, even scales, nuanced pedaling and lyric phrasing.

Since my tuition was free, I wanted to take as many classes as I could and learn as much about everything I found of interest as possible. I took chemistry and physics. I took calculus and despised the difficulty of this higher mathematics. As I liked to quip, "I'm a musician and we just count to four and start over again." My struggles with calculus were a disappointment to my grandfather, but he seemed pleased with my insatiable desire to learn. I had a wonderful history professor and my biology and genetics classes were also very enjoyable. But music stole my heart, and I wanted to become a professional pianist.

My grandfather strongly disfavored this idea, and he knew how to reason with his horse-crazy granddaughter. "How will you provide for Sam, if you're just a musician?" he asked. My solution was to major in both music and science. Grandpa never doubted my ability to do well in both areas of study, but my faculty advisor hit the roof.

"You have to CHOOSE! One or the other! Not both!" she sternly admonished me in her smoker's raspy voice.

"But why? Why must I choose?" Having waited so many years to have access to private instruction, I was loathe to give up my piano lessons.

"Well, for one thing, you haven't taken any foreign language. Now you're behind if you want to double-major, and I don't see how you'll ever catch up."

"What if I get permission from an instructor to double up courses and try to catch up that way?"

"They'll never agree to such a plan," she scoffed.

"But what if they do?" I persisted.

"Then I'll consider your request."

Fueled either with the fearlessness of youth or the determination of the successful, I approached one of the professors who taught German. German II was being offered during the upcoming semester, but I had not taken German I, a prerequisite to German II. And I needed German II to enroll the following semester in German III. And I needed all three semesters of German to complete my foreign language requirement to get the double-major.

My plan was to ask the professor if I could enroll in German II and, simultaneously, study German I as an independent study course. It was a novel approach to jumping into a sequential course, and he was intrigued.

"Did you study German in high school?" he asked.

"No, sir."

He was an elegant scholar, fit and trim, with his spine unbent despite years of reading, studying, and teaching. He looked like a sea captain, with close-cropped silver hair and a tidy silver beard along his firm jaw. He studied me thoughtfully. "So, you've had absolutely no foreign language of any kind, at any time in your education, is that correct?"

"That's correct, sir." I noted his brow start to gather in a frown and I quickly continued, "But I'm a hard worker and if you'll allow me to do this, I promise I'll catch up to your German II students. I won't hold the class back at all, and within just a few weeks, you'll never be able to tell I didn't have German I like everybody else."

"And why is it so important to you to obtain both an Associate of Science and an Associate of Music while you're here?"

"Because I have a horse, sir, and my grandfather says I won't be able to support myself as a musician, let alone keep my horse. And I won't sell Sam, sir, so I really need to get the Associate of Science, as well."

"Don't you have plans to continue your education to the Bachelor level, at least?"

"I hope to, sir, but I want to start by completing both these associate degrees. I've been taking the maximum number of hours they allow each semester."

Surprised, he asked, "Why? Most students prefer to take the minimum requirements!"

"Because it's all *free*!" I couldn't keep the excitement out of my voice. "I am learning about so many different things! Things I never knew about before! And it's all included in my tuition!"

"So you're on scholarship?" he asked.

"Yes, sir. My high school GPA qualified me for an academic scholarship."

He sat back in his chair and steepled his fingertips together as he quietly studied me.

"Well, studying a foreign language can be very challenging. I've never had a student ask to take two levels of

German simultaneously. I'm intrigued by your request." He paused again, and then his ice blue eyes twinkled.

"I like a challenge. Here's what we'll do. Plan to spend an hour in my office each week for the first few weeks, and I'll give you private tutoring sessions to help you catch up. If you're doing well enough by the last day of drop/add, I'll let you stay in German II. Fair enough?"

"Fair enough!"

Later, I heard whispers in the hallways that my advisor and the German professor had had a rather heated exchange regarding his unorthodox approval of my request. But I was allowed to enroll in German II and had an independent study course number assigned for German I. That semester, I carried a twenty-five hour course load and worked two jobs to pay for Sam.

I bought the course textbook on German and made notecards to practice the basic vocabulary. I kept a few notecards in my pocket to practice anytime I had a few moments, but mostly, I practiced out loud down in Sam's pasture. I would groom him and count the brush strokes out loud, "ein, swei, drei, vier, funf, sechs, sieben, acht, neun, zehn." I would make rudimentary sentences and tell Sam how beautiful he was, "Du bist ein schones Pferd." During my tutoring sessions, my professor would correct my errors, "Sie sind ein schones Pferd."

The last day to drop or add a class came, and my professor called me into his office after class.

"I confess, I was totally skeptical at the beginning," he said. "I honestly didn't think it was possible to jump into a language without the requisite vocabulary and preliminary study and not be left behind." He paused, and smiled his sea-captain bearded smile. "But I'm absolutely delighted with your progress. I've never seen anything like it, to be frank.

You're actually ahead of many of the other pupils, and I'm delighted to allow you to stay in German II. I don't think we even need any more tutoring sessions, but I'm always available if you have a question about the course, at either level."

While some might scoff at the notion of being proud of graduating from a community college, I can say my associate degrees—Associate of Music and Associate of Science, remain two of the proudest academic achievements of my lifetime.

Chapter Twelve

The time came for me to move forward in my academic studies, and that meant the University of Tennessee in Knoxville. That started out as quite a commute, but eventually, Sam and I found ourselves in East Knox County, and he enjoyed lazy days while I continued my education. A combination of Pell grants and academic scholarships funded my university tuition, and I was grateful to continue keeping my word to my mother that I would scholarship my way through school.

Without doubt, the scariest part of moving from the local community college to UT was my placement audition for the piano faculty. There were three professors in the piano department of the UT School of Music. One was a delightful lady who was warm and sincere as a human being, and incredibly gifted as a musician and as a teacher. One was a Yale scholar who intimidated me a little bit with his aggressive but brilliant style. The third had graduated from Columbia University. His teaching lineage was unbroken all the way back to Beethoven. He had been a pupil of Julliard's Adele Marcus, who studied with Artur Schnabel, who studied with Franz Liszt, who studied with Czerny, who was one of Beethoven's pupils. This man's name was William Dorn. He was a portly man of German descent, with piercing blue eyes and silver hair.

My community college teacher had been a Dorn pupil, and she told me when I went to UT that I should request to study with Mr. Dorn. The first time I ever saw Mr. Dorn was at one of his pupil's recitals. Her name was Lisa, and she was a slender, beautiful blonde, who could make the piano sing. Her gown was lovely under the bright stage lights of the UT Concert Hall. I'd never been in a recital hall before. It seemed vast, with its hundreds of plush seats on the sloping floor. Lisa played like the artist she was, and Mr. Dorn was pleased with her performance. As I shyly approached them after the concert in order to introduce myself to Mr. Dorn, I overheard him say, "It was really quite good. But you could have nuanced that D-flat just a bit better." I noted his exactness and worried about my meager skills.

My audition was in the lady professor's studio. Two ebony Steinway "B" pianos sat side-by-side in the crowded space, their seven-foot lengths nearly touching the back wall, with barely enough space for a thin person to scoot between each piano. Her desk was in one corner, overflowing with music and papers. The phone was half-covered in an open score.

The Lady, the Yale man, and Mr. Dorn welcomed me and told me to sit down at the first Steinway. They asked about my repertoire. The list was an unimpressive half-page of beginner works—sonatinas and two-part inventions to develop technique. I had no regal Beethoven sonata, no complex Bach fugue, no lyric Chopin ballade, no showy Liszt nor wartime Prokofiev in my resume.

"This is all?" Mr. Dorn's voice fairly dripped with disdain.

"Yes, sir," I quietly replied.

"But you want to *major* in music?" His voice was incredulous.

"Yes, sir," I again responded, not knowing what else to say.

These three highly acclaimed professionals exchanged knowing looks. The Lady finally offered me a smile of encouragement and said, "Please go ahead and play something for us."

I turned my shoulders square to the keyboard and raised my hands to the keys that started my first piece. I took a deep breath and let it out slowly. As I bowed my head and closed my eyes, I caught a glimpse of the elegant gold embedded into the keyboard cover of the piano: "Steinway & Sons." The fancy, scripted, capital "S" letters made me think of Sam. Part of my mind's eye then began seeing each note, phrase, fingering and pedal marking on the audition piece, and my fingers began to play. Another part of my mind's eye saw me and Sam enjoying a lovely stroll in a sunny meadow, and the music began to flow.

I was told later that the Lady's telephone rang sometime during my audition piece. I confess I never heard it. I was in my own world, where Sam and I were walking together while the composer's music flowed all around us. As the final notes whispered away, I placed my hands back in my lap, raised my head, and mentally returned to the Lady's studio. I had no idea how well or poorly I had played. But I had enjoyed the mental stroll with Sam.

"Please wait outside while we discuss your performance," the Lady instructed.

I obeyed and wondered about my future while I wandered up and down the hallway. I noticed that each piano professor's studio had two Steinway "B" pianos. I marveled at what a luxury it would be to have not one, but *two* pianos—and huge, grand pianos at that!

Finally, the Lady's door opened and I was summoned back inside.

The Lady spoke first. "I'm so sorry about the phone, Esther, but you didn't miss a beat—or a note, for that matter. You have an amazing ability to focus, despite any nerves and distractions."

The Yale scholar remained silent.

Mr. Dorn then spoke, "Your repertoire is nearly nonexistent! What makes you think you can start piano lessons as a college freshman and catch up to pupils who have had private instruction since they were, in some cases, five years old?" His voice sounded irritated, like he was somehow personally insulted by my impertinence.

"I know I'm behind —"

His blue eyes grew icy. "Behind? Why didn't your parents have you studying as a child?"

I thought of fried bologna sandwiches and all the years my mother had stayed up until midnight, night after night, grading papers and preparing lesson plans, so she could teach the children of couples with whom she once socialized. Until she divorced and it became unfashionable to socialize with my mother.

My chin raised a notch of its own accord as I answered this descendant-of-Beethoven's-teaching.

"I was raised by my mother. I have two older sisters. There was no money for piano lessons until I got to college and they were included in my tuition."

The Lady frowned a bit at Mr. Dorn and she asked her own question. "So you've only been *playing* since you were eighteen?"

"No, ma'am. My mother plays—church music and beautiful songs from the forties and fifties like Stardust and songs like that. I learned by ear from listening to her. I started playing when I was three years old."

I looked again at Mr. Dorn. Sky blue German eyes and sapphire blue Scottish eyes locked in a silent battle of respect. Here was a formidable, elegant, accomplished professional pianist, and he had knowledge I dearly wanted to obtain. But my mother had done everything she could to protect her children, and feed us, and give us whatever opportunities she could.

She had given me Sam.

Mr. Dorn broke the silence. "Your community college teacher told us that, despite your dearth of training and repertoire, you have an interpretive gift. We agree."

The Lady smiled at me as Mr. Dorn continued.

"I will take you on as a pupil, but there is much to be done. I will give you extra lessons every week, and I expect you to attend each one. You must also practice at least four hours every day."

"Yes, sir!" I happily agreed.

I could hardly wait to tell Sam! I was going to study piano with someone of Beethoven's teaching lineage! That meant, like Thoroughbred racehorses and bloodlines and such, that maybe someday if I practiced hard enough, I, too, would be considered an "offspring" of Beethoven's teaching!

Of course, what I *didn't* tell Mr. Dorn was my plan to continue studying both music *and* science. Throughout my undergraduate studies at UT Knoxville, I carried a maximum course load almost every semester and ended up with three concurrent degrees: a bachelor of music in piano literature and pedagogy, a bachelor of arts in botany, and a bachelor of arts in biology.

Mr. Dorn might never have found out about my triple-major intentions, but for the fact that one day I arrived for my piano lesson late, dressed in damp jeans with muddy hem and a t-shirt. Mr. Dorn insisted his pupils dress "appropriate for the music: "As you practice, so you play, and you should come to your lessons looking like ladies and gentlemen, not bums or hoodlums."

When he saw my disheveled appearance, his disapproval was obvious. "You're late, and you're not properly dressed for a piano lesson!"

"Yes, sir, I know. I'm very sorry."

As he studied my muddy jeans, he couldn't help his curiosity. "Where on earth have you been?"

Busted, I decided to come clean. "Well, sir, um, actually, um, in addition to my music studies, I'm also taking some science classes. I had a field trip early this morning. My class went to the Smoky Mountains to look for salamanders, which took us through some wetlands and streams . . ."

"Why would you take science classes? I thought your community college courses had covered all such liberal arts requirements."

"Well, sir"—I hesitated, not wanting to displease this man who was teaching me so much about the piano and the music I loved to play. "I've finished organic chemistry and the hardest classes. If I take just a few more, I can graduate with three bachelor degrees, sir."

"*Three?* Whatever would you want or need three degrees for?"

By this time, I knew enough about William Dorn to know he had been raised in St. Louis in a three-story home with five servants—an upstairs maid, downstairs maid, cook, gardener, and a chauffeur. Mr. Dorn didn't *need* to work. He taught because he loved the music and he loved teaching. He had never married, had no children, and sometimes justified his lifelong bachelorhood by saying, "The piano is my mistress, and she's very unforgiving."

"Well, sir, one reason is because I will need to make a living once I'm out of school, and I'm not yet sure how I'm going to do that. So I thought it would be wise to cover all my bases, so to speak. But the main reason is I just *love* to learn, and my academic scholarship and Pell grants cover the costs of a full course load, so I want to study hard and take as many classes as I possibly can while I'm in school." I was embarrassed by the enthusiasm in my voice, honest though it might be.

He studied me for a very long time. I grew embarrassed by his silence and I was afraid he would release me as one of his pupils. Finally, he looked again at my dirty clothes and I thought I caught some hint of deepening respect in his eyes. Surely I was mistaken. When he spoke, his voice was formidable. "Do not *ever* come into this studio again in such a state—do you understand?"

"Yes, sir."

"The *music* deserves much better than this!" His disdain was evident.

Later that evening, as I was feeding Sam his supper, I talked with him about my piano professor. "Sam, I think Mr. Dorn gets lonely sometimes. I mean, he was born into privilege and he has had the best of everything. But there are moments when I think he would like to experience more of "real" life, you know? Like maybe he knows he's been sheltered in some ways. That's great for appreciating opera, and, let me tell you, Sam, Mr. Dorn *loves* opera. I don't know how I feel about opera. I like the good singers. But when it's

Esther L. Roberts

bad, it's *really* bad. But I wonder if anybody's ever invited Mr. Dorn to just kick back and order pizza? Or enjoy a chili dog? Or something plain and simple like that."

Sam kept munching his hay while I brushed his coat.

Chapter Thirteen

I remember one day, as I started to enter Mr. Dorn's studio for my piano lesson, the student whose lesson was before mine came out the door and quietly whispered, "He's really uptight today." Curious, yet grateful for being forewarned, I entered my piano professor's studio to find him speaking angrily into the phone.

"This is simply unacceptable," he growled. "My sister is coming in for Christmas, and I'm having a party, and I *must* have outstanding staff to help serve!"

The conversation continued, but to no avail. Mr. Dorn eventually hung up the phone in a huff, his face red and flustered. "How can people run out of staff during the holidays?" He asked to no one in particular.

"Forgive me, sir. I couldn't help but overhear. Is there anything I can do to help out?"

Mr. Dorn looked at me askance. "My sister, Prudence, is coming to visit from San Francisco over the Christmas holidays. I'm having a soirée for some friends, and I'm making my mother's coconut cake, among other things. The hors d'oeuvres trays need to stay full, but the coconut cake is the big thing. I shred the coconut fresh, and the cake is four layers tall, very moist, and fabulous. But it's got to be cut correctly, and in thin slices, and it's very difficult to do properly."

I'd never seen someone so uptight about cutting a cake before. By this time in my life, I had worked in several restaurants, and helped friends serve at various weddings and other events. I figured I could handle cutting a cake.

"Well, I'd be happy to help out, if you want."

"Have you any experience cutting elegant cakes?" He seemed skeptical.

I could well imagine his trepidation, to even consider letting this native of Appalachia—an authentic Tennessee "hillbilly"—into his home. I imagined his home would be something spectacular. After all, didn't Mr. Dorn have a huge, original oil painting of a sailing ship at sea on his studio wall? Each time I came in for a lesson, I admired the spectacular painting with its powerful depiction of an epic struggle between sturdy vessel and tempestuous sea. The various shades of blue, turquoise and emerald waves with their frothy white peaks were beautiful, and the oil was so thick it seemed like the waves leapt off the canvas. Surely, if he had such a painting in his office, his home would be filled with even more spectacular works, and I wondered if he was insulted that I'd even offered to help with his party.

"Well, sir, I've helped serve multi-tier wedding cakes, and I'll do my best."

I guess desperate situations force the mind to consider improbable solutions, but, for whatever reason, Mr. Dorn decided to have me cut the coconut cake.

On the eve of the party, I put on my best dress (navy blue, from JC Penney's, and several seasons old) and some plain navy pumps. I had wished for a brightly colored holiday dress, but my budget didn't provide for such luxuries. I did have some new earrings, though.

A couple of years prior, in a rare moment of spontaneity, I had gotten my ears pierced. My entire earring wardrobe consisted of the original piercing studs, one pair of deliciously tacky red parrot dangles—a gift from my eldest sister on some trip to the beach—and a small pair of round, gold studs which I wore nearly every single day.

I knew a good bit about saddle pads and how wool was better than any synthetic because it wicks sweat away from the horse and helps keep the skin dry and unchafed. I didn't know much at all about fashion or jewelry. But I did know that, for Mr. Dorn's party—what had he called it?—a "swaray" or something close to that, I needed something better than my little gold earrings. So I went to JC Penney's and bought the least expensive pair of pearl studs I could find. They were tiny, but they were real pearls. I didn't realize until much later that they were so small they were "baby" earrings, eensy little seed pearl studs for nearly newborns to wear at their christening or some such. What mattered to me was they were real pearls.

"Sam," I said as I fed him his supper, "I'm going to a very fancy party tonight, over at Mr. Dorn's. I'm just serving, I'm not actually a guest, but at least I'll get to see fine ladies and watch how they hold their teacups." I had another happy thought. "Oooh, Sam! I'll get to see Mr. Dorn's piano! Won't that be a fine thing to see?" Sam was more impressed with his grain than with any chatter about fine china and pianos.

At that time, Sam and I were living on the east side of Knox County, where all the farmers live. Mr. Dorn lived on the west side, in one of the finest neighborhoods in Knoxville. As I drove around the curving, wooded lane by the lake, I looked with awe at the stately homes with their manicured lawns. As it was Christmastime, many homes had twinkling lights adorning the shrubs and trees and along the walkway to the front door. It was a festive sight and I couldn't help but smile.

When I got to Mr. Dorn's home, I parked my rusty pickup truck on the street and gave a small sigh as I climbed out. It wasn't a great truck. It wasn't a new truck. It certainly didn't belong here in this elegant neighborhood. But that's what I drove, *so that's what I drove*. The hinges creaked as I slammed the door. It shuddered in my hand as it latched. Bits of rust broke off the bottom of the door and drifted like tiny orange snowflakes to the pavement at my feet.

His home was a red brick ranch style, two stories, with light turquoise painted shutters alongside every window and a pair of bright red lacquered front doors. The walkway was lined with perfectly manicured ivy and the front landing was slate. I rang the doorbell and heard two perfectly tuned chimes answer in reply. It sounded like someone had taken two pipes from a grand organ and made a doorbell out of it. There were boxwood wreaths adorning the front door, complete with bright red berries woven amongst the boxwood, and red velvet bows with long streamers hanging down. I heard the distinctive "click click click" of a lady's high heels and the door opened to reveal the most elegant female I had ever seen.

"Good evening. I'm Bill's sister, Prudence Dorn. Please come in." Her voice was rich and polished, with every syllable pronounced with distinction. She was very petite. She had pale white skin, perfectly coifed light henna hair, and sparkling blue eyes. Her face was regal, with a hint of kindness.

She wore a lovely black dress with a silk scarf of Christmas red and green wrapped in seemingly effortless folds around her neck. The scarf was secured by a stunning diamond brooch. The brooch was a circle of graduated diamonds, with a larger diamond sitting like the sun along its diamond orbit. I felt like I was meeting royalty.

As I stepped into the slate foyer of the house, I was immediately struck by how well the house fit the lady before me. The entryway was paneled with bleached wood. The living room, to my left, featured white-on-white silk wallpaper and white silk heavy draperies. I looked at the voluminous, ornate design and wondered if my mother, seamstress that she was, could have ever made such elaborate window coverings. At the far end of the spacious living room stood Mr. Dorn's Steinway "B"—with the lid up—a stately testament to the talent of the homeowner. Opera scores and miscellaneous piano music lay in stacks on each side of the piano's music rack; volumes upon volumes of music was semi-hidden behind an oriental screen at the foot of the instrument.

The living room sofa was also white silk. Two blue velvet chairs sat across from the sofa. Other elegant chairs provided ample seating for guests. Large glass lamps (I would later learn they were Waterford crystal) graced the end tables on either end of the sofa.

A live Christmas tree also sat in the living room, decked with old, fragile glass ornaments and strands of large, colored lights.

"This way," Miss Dorn instructed, and I quietly followed her into the dining room. The dining table should have been the main focus of the dining room, but one hardly saw it, despite its massive size and elegant finish, because of the chandelier above it. I stopped abruptly; I was so taken with the overhead light. The fixture was much more than a means to provide light. It was a work of art. Beautiful pieces of crystal hung individually from tiny wires along the frame of the piece. The crystal pieces ranged from heavy, clear glass dangles to colored pieces of fruit—amethyst colored clusters of grapes, amber colored pears, light yellow apples. I'd never seen such a thing before in my life.

Miss Dorn noted my silent study of the piece. "You like it?" she inquired.

"It is beautiful," I replied, the awe evident in my voice.

She smiled. "It's Baccarat. It was created sometime around 1650."

"1650?" I couldn't suppress my amazement. "That's back in Bach's time!"

"Yes," she replied, as though it were the most normal thing in the world to have a three-centuries-old Baccarat chandelier hanging in one's dining room.

I willed my attention away from the fascinating fixture and looked around the room.

The dining table was overloaded with fancy delicacies. I had no clue what many of them were called, let alone what they were made of. Standing proudly at one end of the table, however, was my date for the evening. The coconut cake.

It looked to be eight inches tall; pure white icing covered in freshly grated coconut. Even with the table between us, I could smell the fresh coconut. It stood with all its four-tier glory upon a cake stand made of fine china. Beside it was a silver cake service, including both knife and serving piece. A stack of ornate china dessert plates were alongside, as well.

"Please make the slices about one-half inch at the back," Miss Dorn instructed. "That may sound small, but it's very rich."

"And very *tall*," I couldn't help but add, and she smiled.

"Indeed." She studied me for a moment, and then said, "The guests should start arriving before too long. Do you need anything else at the moment?"

"A damp towel, if you don't mind, ma'am," I requested.

"A damp towel?" Her puzzled tone was evident. "Whatever for?"

"To keep the knife edge clean, ma'am. I'll wipe the blade after every cut so it doesn't crumble the edges of any slice."

Her expression of surprise let me know Miss Dorn had never cut her own cakes before.

"I've never heard of that, but it certainly makes sense." She left for the kitchen and returned momentarily with a monogrammed linen napkin, damp to the touch.

I noticed the letter of the monogram. "L?" I mused out loud. I didn't want to be nosey, but it seemed that, since their last name was Dorn, shouldn't the monogram be "D" instead?

I guess my bemusement showed on my face, because Miss Dorn chose to explain.

"The linens were my mother's—Florence Lothman before she married my father and became Florence Dorn—hence the 'L' in the monogram. My own given name is Prudence Lothman Dorn. Mother had so many linen napkins, Bill and I divided them after she passed on. You can't get this quality of linen anymore, so we use them despite the 'L'."

The front doorbell rang, and she turned to answer it, noting as she left, "The guests are starting to arrive. Wait twenty minutes, and then begin cutting the cake."

I noted the time from a small china clock nearby, and watched her walk away, wondering how anyone ever learned to walk in such an elegant manner. She held her small frame erect without being stiff, and she glided across the floor with grace and dignity. She was a noble lady, to be sure, and yet there was a sincerity and a genuineness about her that was immediately evident.

As the food editor for McCall's magazine, Prudence Dorn's career had taken her all around the globe. Since retiring, she had moved to San Francisco and worked with start-up food companies there, helping them with marketing and establishing their brands.

To cut a tall, moist, multilayer cake, one needs a sharp knife with a long, serrated edge. To cut such a cake with large particles in it, such as pecans, raisins, or hand-grated coconut, one must keep the blade spotlessly clean. So, after each cut, one gently wraps a moist cloth around the blade, edge out, and swipes the length of the blade. Turn the cloth often and never wipe the blade in the same spot twice.

One cuts, or "plates" a cake one slice at a time. A broad, spade-shaped cake server is slipped vertically into the first knife cut of the cake. As the second cut completes the cake slice, the cake server and knife support the respective sides of the slice while one carefully extracts the slice, places it over the plate, and gently tilts the slice onto its side. The trick, of course, is to mentally configure where the slice needs to be prior to tilting so that, as it is turned on its side, it winds up relatively centered on the plate, preferably without any morsel of cake overhanging the plate, and without the slice falling apart.

A biscuit-maker at a café where I once worked taught me how to slice and serve cakes. I said a silent prayer of gratitude for Lela's instruction as I stood beneath a Bach-era chandelier and served an exquisite dessert to some of the most elegant people I'd ever seen.

My Friend Sam

The gentlemen were, to a man, dressed in dark suits, crisp white shirts, and silk ties. Their shoes were the only thing that was even remotely familiar to me, as they were constructed of leather. But every wingtip was spotlessly polished and gleamed under the soft light of the Baccarat. These men were the artistic elite, the creative aristocracy of Knoxville. When compared to the creative genius that has pervaded such cities as London and Paris for centuries, that appellation, "the creative aristocracy of Knoxville" may seem pathetic, but these gentlemen could discuss the nuances of Berlioz and Bartok, Chopin and Copland as well as any.

It was the ladies, however, who drew, and kept, my covert attention throughout the evening. As I carefully placed an ornate china plate with a dainty slice of coconut cake into each elegant hand, I noted the long, slender fingers and carefully manicured nails. Many of the ladies wore stunning jewelry, and I couldn't help but observe that there seemed to be a direct correlation in one respect. Miss Dorn, with a refined, quiet manner, wore a very modest amount of jewelry, even though the stones were dazzling: diamond earrings, a diamond necklace, and one ring on her right hand.

The ladies most like Miss Dorn—the ones who spoke in soft conversation and seemed to enjoy listening as much as they did talking—they, too, wore brilliant pieces, but limited their adornments to earrings, a necklace or bracelet, and a ring or wedding set.

There were other ladies present, however, who spoke rather loudly and seemed to adore getting everyone's attention focused on themselves. These ladies, whose evening gowns were the colors of prom dresses and hung like they were made of polyester, wore *lots* of jewelry. Huge, dangling earrings and oversized necklaces, stacks of bracelets and rings on nearly every finger. My instinctive desire to favor my hostess made me want to think she had the better taste, but, in truth, I had no idea.

Miss Dorn's gown was black lace over a black silk lining. I had not been around much silk before, but I could tell from how the gown *sounded* as she glided across the room, that there was no polyester involved. There was no loud, "*swoosh, swoosh*" like the taffeta underskirts of my mother's Eastern Star dresses. Miss Dorn's dress barely whispered—"*shss, shss*"—as she walked. I was fascinated by the way Miss Dorn walked. I'd never seen anyone literally *glide* across a room before! Her head didn't go up and down with each stride. Indeed, she seemed legless when she moved, like she was standing on some tiny hovercraft under her gown and, whenever she desired to go from one place to another, the hovercraft simply floated her to her new location.

I studied Miss Dorn's face in surreptitious glances throughout the night. She wore just a bit of eye makeup, blush, and some bright red lipstick, and her hair was carefully coifed in soft curls around her face. I'd never worn makeup in my life. My two elder sisters had done all that "girlie" stuff when we were growing up, but I had had no interest in such things. I had Sam, and he couldn't care less whether I wore makeup. My hair hung in a long, straight, honey-colored waterfall down my back. My mother had always trimmed the ends for me, and no one else had ever touched scissors to my hair. I used cheap shampoo, didn't own a blow dryer, and never thought twice about leaving my apartment each morning with dripping wet hair, straight out of the shower. It was generally dry by the time I got to school and definitely dry by my second class.

Once the cake was served, I kept myself busy with pouring cups of punch and discreetly refilling ornate silver trays with hors d'oeuvres. I stayed quiet beyond the basic necessities of serving the guests. My granddaddy had taught me that folks *teach* by talking, but they *learn* by listening, and I knew I had a lot to learn. So I listened.

Not to the private conversations, and not to any conversation for its substance. I listened to *how* these elegant people spoke. English, as they spoke it, was like a foreign language to my hillbilly ears. Now, in fairness to my Appalachian heritage, of which I'm extremely proud, I'd wager to this day there wasn't a one of those fine folk who could say, "y'all" properly. But that wasn't the point. The point was, I was hearing my native language spoken with a preciseness I'd never heard before. They said, "going" not "goin'." The ladies' laughter was not the raucous haw-hawing of a country family's covered dish dinner. It was soft and bubbly. For the ladies tastefully dressed, like Miss Dorn, it was also sincere.

Southern-born females may not know some things, but one thing we've known for generations is how to detect an insincere female. So when one of the loud ladies, wearing a bright-colored, prom-taffeta dress and dripping with what might have been costume jewelry, came up to Mr. Dorn, wrapped her arms around him (nearly spilling red punch down his crisp white shirt and silk tie) and squealed with her best stage voice, "BILL! How *wonderful* to see you!" instantly, I knew her type:

Tacky.

Chapter Fourteen

The last guest left and the house grew instantly quiet. Mr. and Miss Dorn thanked me for my help and Miss Dorn kindly said, "You did an outstanding job serving this evening, Esther." She was a remarkably astute woman, and was gracious enough not to start babbling like she might have to a society girl: "Your mother must entertain all the time" or some such. Pru Dorn was nobody's fool, and she could tell from the cut of my dress to the scuffed heels of my shoes that my background did not include fancy parties on a regular basis. I didn't have to say a word for her to know *this* was my very first fancy party. Ever. And, most likely, my last.

Mr. Dorn held out his hand to me as I started out the door. "Here, take this, with my thanks." He pressed a folded twenty-dollar bill into my hand. I glanced at Miss Dorn, embarrassed that she should see me take money like a hired hand. My cheeks flushed crimson as I realized that was, in truth, exactly what I had been for the evening. A hired servant. Nothing more. And Sam needed horse feed soon. "Thank you, sir."

I took the cash as Mr. Dorn's other hand closed around mine. I found my hand caught gently between my piano professor's hands, in a silent gesture of thanks for a job well done. It didn't last long, but the contact was long enough for me to realize I was being touched by hands that had played Rachmaninoff's Second Piano Concerto to rave reviews. These were hands of a master artist. Hands that could make the most massive Steinway in the world whisper, or shout, or sing or weep. Hands that had never known a single minute of hard labor. Mr. Dorn's hands had never chopped down fence posts, strung wire, or saddled a horse. Those warm, strong, gentleman's hands had never held a muddy hoof and cleaned the muck from the sole of the foot. Mr. Dorn's hands had never patiently removed cockleburs from a tangled mane. With all his travels and all his education and all his wealth, he'd never touched a horse.

As my teacher removed his clasped hands to open the door, and I walked out in the cool, dark night to my truck, I wondered if Mr. Dorn had a best friend, like my dear Sam was for me.

When I walked into Mr. Dorn's studio at my next piano lesson, I decided to take a calculated risk. "I have a question."

Mr. Dorn knew me well enough by this time to know I had an insatiable curiosity to learn, and I knew him well enough to know he wouldn't mind if I asked some non-music type questions.

He turned his head slightly to one side, his silver hair shining under the fluorescent lights of the studio, and his light blue eyes contemplating his rather unique pupil as she stood before him. "Yes?"

I hesitated a moment, looking up at him and wondering if I was about to cross some social line of etiquette that I didn't even know existed—if it did. Mr. Dorn stood about 5'10", so he wasn't a tall man. But his presence more than made up for any lack of height. He could be the most formidable monument of humanity one might ever hope to cross. Or rather, refrain from crossing, if one were wise. I thought of the Scripture, "The wisdom of men is foolishness to God," and took a deep breath.

"Can you teach me to walk like your sister walks?"

Stunned silence filled the studio. I watched unfathomable emotions cross my professor's face, and I immediately regretted the question, knowing a storm was brewing that would soon unleash its full force in a verbal assault. I wanted to crawl beneath the Steinways and hope one might crash down on me. That would, indeed, be less painful than the wrath of a man I respected and admired so very much.

His blue eyes turned to ice. "What? What did you say?"

I thought of Miss Dorn's breeding and elegance and knew I had grossly overstepped my place. And yet my voice came again, seemingly of its own accord.

"I want to learn to walk like a lady—like your sister." I raised my chin a notch and met his glare, telling myself that my heritage on my mother's side was a long line of teachers and farmers and engineers, smart, hardworking people who always tried to better themselves. But then I recalled the paternal side of my dna and dropped my gaze, knowing I was the daughter of a drunk. A man who had lied to my mother and abused all of us. He had unknowingly killed and maimed others in a drunken stupor behind the wheel. He never even realized he had run a car off the road, so intent was he on entertaining his lifelong passenger, Mr. Jack Daniels. Two people were killed and one was a paraplegic, all because of my paternal dna. I never knew their names, but many lives had been destroyed because of him and his disease. Who was I kidding? I was just a hillbilly who didn't know my place.

I didn't want to look at the floor, but I couldn't look at my teacher, so I chose to focus on the lovely painting of the ship at sea on the wall. That painting was so full of movement and energy, yet it always made me feel calm and at peace. Perhaps that's why Mr. Dorn kept it in the studio; it was very similar to the pianos we played. Strong. Powerful. And yet the source of great serenity to many of us. Or torment, on a bad day. I knew this lesson was going to be one of those "bad day" types. I had angered my teacher.

After what felt like forever, Mr. Dorn asked his own question. "Why? Why do you want to learn this?" I was astounded at the tone of his voice. There was no contempt. There was no ridicule. I couldn't quite pinpoint the emotion underlying his words, but for a fleeting moment I thought I heard, of all things, *awe*.

"Well, it's just that" I stammered, trying to find the words, then rushed into a babbling explanation. "Your sister, um, Miss Dorn, is such an *elegant* lady, and my Aunt Gorda is sort of like that, but she's the only person I've ever seen that's like that, and she lives in North Carolina and I don't get to see her very often and when I watched your sister at the party the other night, she just *glided* across the room and I would *so* love to learn to walk like that and feel like a real lady!" I dammed the torrent of words and stood silent again.

Ice blue eyes studied sapphire blue eyes for a long moment, and then the ice melted and my professor spoke, using his most refined tone and distinct elocution, as though he was speaking to royalty.

"And so you shall, my dear, so you shall."

I beamed with delight. "Thank you!" I stifled the urge to wrap my arms around his neck and hug him in gratitude. In hindsight, I must have looked like an eager puppy, fairly wriggling with excitement, but trying to obediently stand still and be a good girl.

"Well, then,"—once again he was all business—"I'll not take your music lesson time to teach you such things. You're still very behind in your repertoire, despite all the extra lessons, so we'll have to make another schedule to teach you things other than music. You will come to the studio first thing every morning. We shall start tomorrow."

And with that, we turned our immediate attention to Czerny and Bach.

Chapter Fifteen

The following morning, I arrived at the studio door promptly. Mr. Dorn was already there. "Follow me," he bade, and we exited the music building and across the walkway into the neighboring structure, which was the Art and Architecture building. This structure, known across campus as, "A&A" was a massive, multi-storied concrete building with an open atrium in the middle where one could stand and look up, up, up to the skylights above. I found the grey concrete walls to be austere and uninspiring, but there were multiple stairways of brightly painted steel criss-crossing the perimeters of the atrium, which broke up the drabness. The plain grey walls made a fabulous backdrop for the huge canvasses that were periodically hung up to display the students' latest works, and sometimes faculty paintings, as well. Several welded sculptures that were beyond my ken were on display throughout the building. To my unsophisticated eye, more often than not these works of art looked more like someone had taken a rusty tractor out of a local farmer's field, taken it apart, and then welded it back together all askew and completely void of rhyme or reason. I recall one in particular, with the ochre-colored metal seat now attached at an insane angle to the oil-stained steering rod, with various gears and bolts welded all about. An oversized bloom for Frankenstein's bride, perhaps? I had no idea. But the A&A building was always interesting.

It was also always noisy, with the painted concrete floors bouncing every conversation all around the glass ceiling and concrete walls. To a musician's ears, it was a cacophony of sound, and I wondered how Mr. Dorn could tolerate the aural madness, yet he appeared quite oblivious to the auditory assault.

In the middle of the atrium was a small snack shop, where one could purchase a pastry and hot coffee or tea or a coke. Mr. Dorn, not being from the South, always called carbonated beverages, soft drinks or soda pop, which sounded really weird to me. Anything with carbonated water was known as a coke; one then specified what type of coke—Coca-Cola, Diet Coke, 7-Up, Dr. Pepper.

I rarely ever came to A&A, and even more rarely purchased anything from the snack shop, despite how moist and chewy the freshly made date bars were, with their crumb-cake top and the sweet dates folded inside buttery pastry, or the homemade pumpkin bread, with its delightful blend of spices that spread across your tongue with a flavor so rich and full, you didn't know which ingredient to identify first. Pumpkin and cinnamon and nutmeg and oh, so delicious! A slice of pumpkin bread and a coke was over $2.00, and I didn't have money for such treats very often.

But I meekly followed Mr. Dorn to the A&A snack shop, and stood silently praying I could scrounge up enough coins in the bottom of my purse to buy something—anything! Obviously, my first lesson in how to walk like a lady somehow involved food, and I was going to have to order something.

My Friend Sam

As I silently studied the modest menu, looking for the cheapest thing, I was surprised to hear Mr. Dorn say, "Two date bars, and two cups of hot tea, please."

He paid for our treat and then turned to me and said, "You take the bag; I'll get the cups." We sat down at a small café table with two metal chairs and he handed me my tea. I looked at the strong, black brew, hoping I could drink its bitterness without any sugar. I was too afraid of offending my benefactor to go back to the snack bar and ask for a packet.

"In order to walk like a lady," he spoke as he unwrapped a date bar and gently placed it in front of me, "One must learn to *think* like a lady; refined actions must always begin with refined thought." Upon hearing this, I quickly set the date bar I had just picked up back down, unsure how to eat it without doing something wrong. I had intended to hold it in my hand like a cookie and take an ample bite of its succulent sweetness into my hungry and salivating mouth. Instead, I turned a puzzled but quiet expression to my teacher.

He took note of my actions and smiled. "You listen very carefully, and very well, Esther. This is one reason why I agreed to teach you piano, let alone anything beyond that—because you know how to *listen*. That's a rare gift; I just don't see it in many pupils anymore." Unaccustomed to praise, I continued to sit silently watching him, taking note of his every movement.

He unwrapped his date bar and left it sitting on the waxed paper, then gently raised an edge and broke off a small piece, and brought it to his mouth. Ah! Now I knew what to do, so I did the same thing. Or I tried to. My grip was too harsh and I mashed the corner of the treat. Crumbs scattered across the table and into my lap. My thumb and forefinger had gooey date filling on them, and I *knew* I couldn't lick my fingers, but I hated to waste that sticky richness! Sighing silently at the wasted goodness, I wiped my fingers and tried again, this time with better success.

Unsweet tea is a foreign substance to many Southerners, and I was no exception. We Southerners drink iced tea, not hot tea, and we drink it sweet. *Very* sweet. At that point in my life, I had not sampled elegant teas from various parts of the world, and the economy-pack tea served by a public university in the southern United States was hardly a good introduction into the rich and flavorful world of hot tea. This tea was over brewed and black as pitch in its unceremonious paper cup. The sides of the cup were so hot I could hardly lift it without burning my fingertips, and pianists prefer unburned hands, generally speaking. But Mr. Dorn sipped his tea without a fuss, so I did my best to follow suit. It was bitter and awful, yet the next bite of date bar seemed even more flavorful after the unsweetened beverage. Interesting.

As we sat, eating and drinking, Mr. Dorn began to point out some of the female students who walked by. "See that girl, how she takes such long steps and bounces up and down with every stride? She is taking strides too long for her own body, and doesn't even realize it. She's in too much of a hurry. You must learn to take sufficient *time* to walk like a lady." At my bemused expression, he elaborated. "Don't take a longer stride than you have leg for, my dear. You are not a tall human, so your step must match your leg length. Don't worry about how long it takes you to get from point A to point B. The world will always wait for a lady." He stopped and smiled and corrected himself, "Well, except for planes and ships. They wait for no one, which is a constant source of irritation to my sister, who is perpetually late for everything."

My Friend Sam

I couldn't help but smile at his mild annoyance with his sibling. The idea of Mr. Dorn, piano professor extraordinaire, being irritated with his sister, was so provincial, so *ordinary*, it made both of them seem a bit more human.

Seeing me smile, he continued. "My sister was the food editor for McCall's magazine back in its heyday. She lived her life in New York and was in some of the best social circles there. She never married. Her only companion was a blue parakeet she called, Mr. Blue. She had a tiny apartment and it was always chock full of clothes and recipe books and junk!" I could only imagine what Mr. Dorn would consider to be, "junk!" but I stayed silent as he continued to speak. "When she retired, she moved to San Francisco, and she works with food companies out there, helping them with marketing and those types of things."

"She's a very elegant lady."

"That she is, my dear. And so shall you be, if you want it badly enough and you're willing to work very hard."

"I'll do my very best, sir."

"I know you will, else I'd not be bothered with the work we'll have to do."

Our tea and date bars finished, he stood up and I followed his lead. "Now, stand up straight, raise your chin a bit, and don't look at the ground." I did as instructed and jumped ever so slightly when I felt his hand on my shoulder, his grip warm yet firm. "Shoulders back," he spoke quietly, so no one else could hear our subtle lesson in posture. I appreciated his discretion, not wanting the entire student body to know Esther the hillbilly was trying to morph into something she had no right to be.

"Now, take reasonable steps for your leg, don't overstride, and use your hips." The last comment completely puzzled me and I turned to look at him over my shoulder.

"My hips? But isn't it my *feet* that are doing the walking?" He smiled a genuine smile and chuckled as he answered, "Yes, but a lady uses her hips so her head doesn't bounce!" I guess he saw my mind at work, for he added, "Yes, cogitate on that a while and then the physics involved will make sense."

"Cogi-what?"

"Cogitate. Think. Ponder. Digest."

Later that evening, as I brushed Sam to the sound of his rhythmic chewing on fresh hay, I cogitated on how the ball of the foot lifts to carry one forward, thus there is upward motion that has to go somewhere; either by elevating the entire body up and creating the bobbing heads of farmhands as they stride from chore to chore, or by redirecting the upward motion out through the hips with a gentle swing, thus allowing the head and torso to remain relatively level and erect. "It's the same as when I'm riding you, Sam!" I cried with delight! "When you trot forward, my hips swing open to allow your movement to carry us *through* the motion so I don't bounce on your back! That makes sense!"

Of course, understanding theory is one thing. Putting it into practice is quite another, and Mr. Dorn and I spent many days walking to A&A to have tea and a treat. While the food and conversation were always wonderful, the purpose of those daily walks was so he could evaluate my progress in self-carriage. He was, above all, a gentleman, and his instruction was both illuminating and discreet.

Days turned into weeks, and soon Mr. Dorn and I had relaxed a bit in each other's company. He had learned some about my own history, and about Sam, and about how someone like me had dreamed of becoming a lady. I learned about his youth. How his grandparents had come to America from Germany and settled in St. Louis. They had opened a

My Friend Sam

lumber mill right as the west was opening up, so they did a booming business. His mother had inherited wealth, as well, and so young Prudence and Billy Dorn had grown up quite literally with the proverbial silver spoon.

Prudence had been given piano lessons from a tender age, and she wept in despair at every lesson until her mother finally relented and allowed her to cease. Young Billy, however, had begged for lessons and, once instruction had begun, his prodigious talent became evident. Should he grow restless with scales and arpeggios and break out into the new music of the day—jazz—his grandmother Dorn, matriarch of the household, would stand at the upstairs banister and shout at him, "I'll have none of the nonsense in this household! Stop that racket at once and get back to your practicing, Billy!" Even his recounting of the tale made me shudder, so stern was Grossmutter Dorn. It also seemed surreal to hear my piano professor tell of being called Billy. I only knew him as Mr. Dorn, and it seemed strange to my ears to hear his peers refer to him as Bill. To think of anyone, even his family, calling this great artist Billy was nearly beyond comprehension. Later opportunities would affirm this, however, for I have since seen many of his early study piano scores, bound in fine black leather, now cracked with time. Inscribed on each front cover in heavy gold leaf are the words *Billy Dorn*.

Chapter Sixteen

As my walking improved, Mr. Dorn began working on other "rough edges," as he called it. "Do you know the proper use of a fish fork?" He asked me one day.

"What's a fish fork?"

With a heavy sigh, he closed his eyes and gave a small shake of his head. "As I suspected," I heard him murmur under his breath. Then he opened his eyes and looked at me with a thoughtful eye, as one might view a curio on a shelf at an antique store, wondering whether it were some undiscovered treasure or merely a cheap souvenir.

"Have you ever heard the story of Pygmalion?" he asked.

"No, never heard of it."

He studied me a moment more. "How about the musical, *My Fair Lady*?"

"Oh, yes! Audrey Hepburn and her drunken father, and some guy she called her Professor."—I stopped, mid-sentence, as light began to glimmer.

"You shall be my Pygmalion project," he said in an authoritative voice. He began to pace the small space of his studio, back and forth between the two pianos and his desk, pausing at the window to look outside before turning back again. "Yes." He continued pacing, stopping every now and again to study me as I stood near one of the instruments. "Yes!" His voice grew enthusiastic.

"What do you mean, sir?"

"Well, my dear, if you want to be a lady, I shall teach you. Not only how to walk, but how to sit, how to stand, how to walk down the stairs without looking at your feet. How to *dine*. Any animal knows how to *eat*, but civilized people know how to *dine*."

I must have looked very confused, because he explained, "A fine meal should be an event unto itself, not just a quick, 'grab it and growl' fueling session prior to another activity."

"Oh," I replied, although I still had absolutely no idea what he was talking about.

"We shall begin as soon as possible. I will take you to dinner this Friday evening."

I had become comfortable enough with my teacher to ask questions as my curiosity compelled me to do so. "What should I wear?" I asked.

"A dress," he curtly replied.

Friday evening arrived and Mr. Dorn came to my door and rang the bell. I was wearing one of my best Sunday dresses and I hoped he didn't notice the scuff marks on the heels of my pumps. Pickup trucks are not known for luxurious carpeting on the floor, and the rubber floor mats in my truck wreaked havoc on my cheap shoes, as random gravels from my driveway inevitably found their way into the truck, where they ground between my heels and the accelerator and the clutch. I'm guessing the same would have happened with designer heels.

He looked me up and down and I timidly asked, "Is this okay?"

My Friend Sam

A kind light shown in his eye as he replied, "It will do." He escorted me to the passenger's side of his car and set me into the seat as if I were a queen. "Sit first, then swing your feet in; that's how a lady enters a vehicle."

His "vehicle" was a fully loaded Acura sedan, with blue leather seats and burled walnut trim. I'd never seen anything like that car. It was immaculate, yet I knew he hadn't just purchased a new car. "Who keeps their car *this* clean?" I pondered as I relaxed into the comfortable seat. "Ooooh. I hope I can afford to buy Sam a saddle someday that's made of such fine leather," I thought to myself and smiled. I inhaled deeply, wanting to fill my senses with the smell of fine leather. The smell of fine leather, however, was overpowered by the scent of expensive cologne. I nearly gagged as the rich fragrance filled my head, and I did cough aloud as Mr. Dorn climbed into the driver's seat and another wave of his cologne filled the air of our closed environment. "Are you wearing cologne," I tried to hide my distress by a simple question.

"Obsession," he replied. "I love it. It's very expensive. I practically bathe in after every shower."

Truth, for sure.

Bill Dorn was a gifted artist and a brilliant teacher, but one thing he absolutely could not do was drive well. His ear, so acutely aware of every nuance in a musical performance, from the most delicate Mozart sonata to the most bombastic Wagnerian opera, was completely immune to the Acura aria going on beneath his feet. He would accelerate quickly from a stop while the car's rpms shrieked to catch up and his passengers tried to catch their breath from the g-forces that pressed them into the seat and distorted one's head and neck like a roller coaster ride. He would mash on the brakes and lock up the front end of the car, hurling his passengers into the bruising restraint of their seatbelts. And backing up would make even the hardest soul implore the Almighty for mercy and protection.

Mr. Dorn was quick to acknowledge his lack of skill, without any apologies whatsoever. "I was raised with a chauffeur and then lived my entire adult life in New York City before coming to Knoxpatch. If this town were truly civilized, one could either walk to anywhere worth getting to, or the public transportation would be better."

There was always a bit of scalding tone when he spoke of New York and Tennessee in the same sentence, and I often wondered why he came to Tennessee if he found it so repugnant a place. He called Knoxville "Knoxpatch" anytime he was annoyed with the smallness or lack of refinement of the city.

We dined at Red Lobster. Not because they use fish knives there (they don't) and not because it's a high-end restaurant (it isn't). I guess we went there because he felt it was on par with my current level of manners, or lack thereof—or whatever. All I knew was I didn't like fish, and this was going to be a challenging dinner.

"What sort of fish do you enjoy?" he asked once we were seated.

"Um, well, um—I usually only eat Long John Silver's fish. I got sick on shrimp once, and I've not eaten fish since."

"Bah!" he spat, and turned to the waiter and ordered for both of us.

I don't recall what type of fish it was. I only know that when it came, it was white and slathered in butter and lemon and I could see where every rib bone had pressed into the flesh. My grave concern was that at least one bone was left, that it would somehow lodge in my throat, and that I would leave Sam all alone after I died from a punctured trachea.

Mr. Dorn showed me how to take small bites, which was easy since my main goal was to eat as little of the fish as I possibly could, even if it meant going hungry later. Hush puppies, I learned, were not to be taken in hand and popped into one's mouth like an oversized morsel of popcorn, but, rather, carefully cut with a fork and ingested in small bites.

"The tines of the fork must be always exposed," Professor Dorn-Higgins explained. "You must never take so much food upon the fork that it covers the tines, nor stick the fork so far into one's mouth as to devour the tines. Lay the knife on the edge of the plate, don't lay a soiled knife upon the tablecloth, nor lean it against the plate." And on the lesson went.

When I ran out of water and started to ask the waiter to refill my glass, Mr. Dorn quickly corrected me, "Don't you remember when I ordered the meal? A gentleman speaks *for* the lady; when you are with me, you are never to speak to a waiter unless you are saying, 'Thank you.'"

Having been raised by my decidedly single mother, I wondered what ladies do when they were alone.

When the meal was over, I started to stack the dishes in a tidy pile, to make life a little easier on the waitress. By this point in my life, I'd worked at several restaurants myself, and I had both sympathy and empathy for anyone who serves the public their food. To my mind, every young person should have to work in a restaurant for at least a brief period. Humans can be incredibly demanding and outrageous when it comes to their behavior toward wait staff, and it would benefit humanity if everyone had to view that world from the "apron" side. At least, in my opinion.

But, that evening at Red Lobster, when I began stacking the dishes, Professor Dorn-Higgins nearly had an apoplectic fit! "What are you *doing*?" he fairly bellowed.

"Stacking the dishes, to help the waitress out a bit," I replied.

"Patrons never—*never*—touch the dishes, and ladies most especially do not!" His voice had become so loud a few people around us looked in our direction, and I wanted to crawl under the table, not only for drawing attention to myself due to Mr. Dorn's anger, but also for not knowing any better than to stack dishes.

That first dinner outing soon became a standing Friday night lesson in dining. I was grateful, not only for Mr. Dorn's willingness to try and make a lady out of such raw material, but also for the good meals. As I learned, the restaurants got better.

Oddly enough, so did my riding. I generally rode Sam on the weekends, since schoolwork and piano practice and various part-time jobs took most of my weekday hours. I saw Sam every morning and every evening, to feed him and do chores, but still, we didn't have a lot of time to just relax and ride during that time. So, when I did get to ride, it was always a treat. And, slowly, I began to feel differently in the saddle. My posture improved, both at the piano, and on my horse. Good posture—straight but not stiff—puts one's seatbones down into the saddle, which stabilizes the rider, and a balanced rider makes the horse's job of carrying a human much easier. And it's always, always, all about the horse. In similar fashion, good posture anchors the seat on the piano bench, so the whole body is free to interact with the instrument. The pelvis acts as a universal joint, so to speak, so the torso and arms and hands are free to move about the keyboard and create nuanced sound, while the legs and feet are available for balance and sensitive pedaling. Who knew horseback riding and classical piano study could be so similar?

Chapter Seventeen

"Makeup!" I snarled one evening as I brushed Sam's coat until it gleamed dark ochre in the fading sun. "Now he thinks I should try wearing *makeup*!" The brush strokes grew firmer as my agitation grew. "*You* don't wear makeup," Sam turned a tolerant eye toward me. He understood my emotions very well, and always listened patiently. "If God wanted me to have purple eyelids, He would have *made* them purple!"

Throughout my girlhood, I had staunchly refused to wear makeup, despite being raised in a family of females. My mother could put on her "war paint"—her term for the claret colored lipstick she wore irrespective of season or outfit—driving forty miles per hour down the steep, winding descent of Wheeler Street. She used face cream, foundation, and blush, I knew. I don't recall her ever using anything on her eyes. My two elder sisters were well versed with makeup, hairstyles, nail polish, and fashion. Well, okay, maybe it was the local "fashion" from JC Penney in downtown Rockwood, or for special occasions, the high end store, Bernards, run by a local Jewish family who always closed the store on Saturdays and everyone was fine with that. Still, my sisters looked at makeup advertisements in magazines and experimented with the latest trends.

Me? I wore jeans every day except Sunday, no makeup whatsoever, and my hair was long and straight and I never bothered with a blow dryer. I was completely oblivious to walking into school with damp hair and a flannel shirt. Even on prom night—no makeup, plain hair. I just never thought about it.

Now, however, I was in college, Mr. Dorn had begun a transformation, and he was extremely intent on his task. He was nearly as clueless as I was with respect to makeup, however, so, unbeknownst to me, he contacted The Expert on All Things Ladylike.

His spinster sister, Miss Prudence Dorn.

Apparently, they had numerous conversations about me in the beginning. Having lived most of her life in New York City, Miss Dorn knew all about fashion and hairstyles and makeup. The only trouble was, Miss Dorn shopped at Neiman Marcus and Bergdorf Goodman's. That, of course, was out of the question; I was merely an "interesting experiment" and not worth such an investment.

Mr. Dorn knew I had no money for such luxuries as high fashion and makeup. So one day in his studio, he handed me an envelope and said, "I've spoken with my sister. We think you should try using some makeup. She said with your skin and hair color, you should look for blush and such with peachy-pink undertones, and use brown mascara and eyeliner instead of jet black."

Inside the envelope was five twenty-dollar bills. "That should be sufficient to get you started."

"This should be more than enough, sir. I'll bring you any change back, I promise."

"Oh, don't worry about the change!" he rather gruffly replied.

"Are you sure about that?" I asked.

"Absolutely!" His tone ended any further discussion. His generosity was overwhelming.

At that point in my life, one hundred dollars was a huge amount of money, and I could hardly believe anyone would spend such an amount on makeup! One hundred dollars could feed me and Sam for weeks! Yet I wanted to be obedient to this gentleman and his sister, who were trying so very hard to help me improve myself. At the same time, I didn't want to slather layer upon layer of foundation and powder and blush and whoknowswhatelse on my skin. I clearly recalled my sisters' face towels in the evenings after they had removed their makeup. Various shades of browns and pinks and stains of black mascara were dreadful to see on a towel—how much worse, then, surely were they on one's *skin*! Ick!

Feeling stuck, I went home that evening and talked it over with Sam. "I have no idea where to begin! I have no idea what store to go to!" I had vague recollections of aisle upon aisle of makeup at the local drug stores. It was beyond my imagination to consider going to those polished chrome stands at the department stores where perfectly made-up sales ladies stood waiting to help you purchase an entire collection of their particular brand. "I dunno, Sam, I don't think I can do this." Sam stood, as always, patiently listening while munching his evening hay. Seeing the calm in his steadfast eye, I sighed. "Okay, okay, I'll do my best."

With trepidation, I climbed in my pickup and drove to the one place I thought I might be able to shop rather inconspicuously—Walgreens. I loved Walgreens. It was small enough to get in and out of quickly, yet it carried an interesting variety of all sorts of things, from deodorant to dog food, greeting cards to girl supplies, milk to makeup.

Inside the store, it seemed there were a million little cardboard packets hanging on two aisles, with shades in every color of the rainbow. The lady pictured on the "L'Oreal" display looked like *she* was, "worth it," but I wasn't sure I was. The "Max Factor" display featured a lot of beige and dark colors. No pinks or peaches. I closed my eyes and tried to recall all the basketsful of makeup my sisters had kept in the bathroom when we were growing up. The only thing I clearly recalled was tubes of mascara—bright pink and lime green. I spied that same tube under the display, "Maybelline." Great Lash. Ah! Something familiar. I studied the packets carefully and quickly learned mascara comes in various colors, including shades of black and brown. I selected brown and decided if Maybelline was good enough for my sisters, it should do just fine for me.

Unsure of what to get, I selected a compressed powder blush, some blue and grey eye shadow, brown eyeliner, the brown mascara, and some pinkish lipstick. When I checked out, my total makeup bill was less than thirty dollars. As I pocketed over seventy dollars in change, I whispered a heartfelt prayer of gratitude. Not only did I have the makeup I had promised to buy, but I had enough money to feed Sam *and* put gas in my truck for a whole month!

The next day, I dutifully stood in front of the mirror and applied the makeup as best as I could. I put grey eyeshadow on the edges of my eye, and blue in the middle. Applying the mascara felt really awkward and I smudged it at least three times and wiped it off to try again. Only the lipstick seemed relatively easy—I'd spent many years watching my mother put her "war paint" on as we drove down Wheeler Street. But it felt sticky and gummy and very foreign on my mouth, and I felt like a circus clown when I surveyed the results in the mirror. "I sure don't *feel* like a lady." I climbed in my truck and drove to school.

When I met Mr. Dorn for morning tea, he studied my face a moment and commented, "The grey and blue eyeshadows go well with your eyes." After we were finished with our daily visit, he noted, "You'll want to reapply your lipstick. But never in public—my sister always excuses herself and steps to the ladies' room to reapply her lipstick." I didn't bother telling him I hadn't thought to bring it with me.

As I moved through the hallways of the music building from class to class, for the first time, I paid attention to the other girls' faces and looked with newfound respect upon some of the colors and shadings on their skin. Mentally comparing my efforts to theirs, I thought perhaps I had been rather successful in my first attempt at applying makeup. Some folks looked at me with mild curiosity, but no one was laughing. Or so I thought.

Mid-morning, I rounded a corner to come upon three other piano students, all of whom began to laugh as I overheard one make some comment about "cat eyes." I hurriedly ducked into the nearest women's bathroom and looked in the mirror. To my horror, I realized that, while all the other girls stopped their eyeliner at the outside corner of their eyelid, I had carefully drawn full lines with the eyeliner pencil from the inside corner of my eye to the outside of my eyebrow! Cat eyes, indeed! Quickly, I tried to wipe the ridiculously-too-long pencil lines out. The dark brown lines simply smudged into the grey eye shadow, making my eyelids turn muddy brown. As I wet a paper towel and tried to wash the mud off, my embarrassment grew to epic proportions as the most beautiful girl in the music program walked into the bathroom—*Lisa!* Why *her*? Why *now*? I was on the verge of tears.

Our eyes met in the mirror and we studied each other's face silently. I have no idea what she saw, but I saw an accomplished musician housed in a model's body, complete with a model's face, flawlessly made up, with equally flawless blonde hair styled in a very high-fashion cut. She was also a Dorn student—the best of his current pupilage—and his current favorite, as well. Lisa had a spare key to Mr. Dorn's studio. Unlike the rest of us who practiced downstairs in the student practice rooms on well-worn pianos, Lisa practiced in Mr. Dorn's studio late in the evenings after he had finished teaching for the day. She was elegant and polished in every way. Lisa was "the whole package," as Mr. Dorn used to say, and he was right.

I bit my lip, willing myself not to cry in front of this gorgeous, talented young woman. Having the mediocre piano students make fun of me was bad enough, but to have someone like Lisa make fun of me would put me straight over the edge. Her eyes never left mine as she spoke in a matter-of-fact tone. "Don't you just hate it when your makeup smears?" I didn't reply.

Lisa set her handbag on the edge of the sink and pulled out a brightly colored makeup bag, fairly bursting at the seams. She unzipped the bag and began sorting through the contents. "Here," she said, and handed me a compact. "And here," some eyeliner followed the compact. She glanced at me in the mirror with savvy eyes.

"You're doing fine, Esther, and folks are starting to notice the difference. *I* can tell the difference in your playing. So ignore all those wannabes and focus on becoming the best *you* you can be, okay?"

"But it seems like I fumble every new thing I try!" My frustration was evident in my voice.

"You think I look this good when I first get up in the morning? God, no! You should see my makeup at home—this is just my emergency kit!"

She flashed me a bright, co-conspirator's grin. "Makeup is just like playing the piano; it just takes daily practice. Now, you hold this stuff for me, and I'll teach you a few application tricks."

Ten minutes later, I walked out of the bathroom with a fresh face and a new friend.

Chapter Eighteen

As I progressed, Mr. Dorn and I learned more about one another. He invited me to his home when Miss Dorn visited the next time. The three of us were to have dinner together. Instead of serving coconut cake, however, this time, I was the guest.

I was invited into the oversized living room with the Steinway sitting proudly at the far end. The gleaming ebony satin finish was a stark contrast to the ivory silk wallpaper on the walls. "The silk wallpaper was a gift from my mother when I built this house," Mr. Dorn said. He loved his living room. Heavy silk draperies covered every window. "I rarely ever open the draperies," he explained, "due to the artwork."

Indeed, his collection of art was unlike any I'd ever seen. Oriental art tastefully covered every wall and shelf. On one wall, a painting on silk of three boys playing with a cat was, "several centuries old." Ancient vases and brightly colored, ornate plates were displayed throughout the house. I later learned the entire collection had its own insurance policy and, in the event of Mr. Dorn's passing, the collection was to be donated to the Birmingham Museum of Art.

My Friend Sam

The living room sofa was eight feet long, with down-filled cushions and covered in white silk. Ornate chairs covered in various patterns of white and blue silk were arranged in an orderly manner around the room. Over to one side, a pair of blue velvet chairs sat in a cozy conversational setting, with a small table between—just the right space for two friends to chat over tea. All in all, it was a marvelous room, as elegant and sophisticated as its owner.

Mr. and Miss Dorn wore cordial hosts and they asked me questions about my studies and such. Mr. Dorn mentioned to his sister that I had a horse named Sam. I spoke with enthusiasm about my beloved pet, and, being animal lovers themselves, we found common ground for relaxed conversation during dinner.

"You learned to ride on a *cow*?"

"Yes, Miss Dorn, a black baldie named Tammy. My grandfather kept a few cows for beef, but he never slaughtered Tammy. She became the family pet when I was a very small child, and Grandpa would put several of us grandkids up on Tammy's back and lead us around."

Miss Dorn was surely pleased with my progress or something about me, because she went so far as to say, "Please, Esther, there's no need to be formal; please call me Pru."

Baby carrots and asparagus were the vegetables of the evening. I had never eaten asparagus before, so I carefully watched the Dorns to see how to cut it and eat it. Carrots, however, were comfortably known to me, and I quickly and carefully sliced up my serving into bite-sized portions.

The next day, over our morning tea, I was excited. "Your sister said I can call her, Pru! Isn't that wonderful?"

Mr. Dorn studied his tea a moment before answering. "Pru mentioned the carrots," he said reluctantly.

"They were delicious! Did you glaze them or something?" In my excitement, I failed to catch the hesitation in his voice.

"Yes, in brandy and brown sugar," he replied, "but that's not the point. You cut your entire serving of carrots up at one time. You must learn to cut *one* bite of food, set down your knife, place the food in your mouth, chew and swallow, then pick up your knife and cut off the next bite. One bite at a time, do you see?"

"I'm so very sorry, sir." I was mortified that, after all our months of working together, I had disappointed him in this first dinner with his sister—with *Pru*.

"It's okay. We'll just work harder." He studied me with a kind eye. "Come on; time to focus on Bach." And we headed to his studio, the professor and his protégé.

Chapter Nineteen

"Sam, what are we to make of this?" I felt genuine surprise as I displayed a greeting card in front of his large, brown eye. "It says, 'You're like a daughter to me'!" Mr. Dorn had signed it, "Fondly, Bill." I had never received mail from him before, and the idea of calling him Bill was nearly unthinkable. Yet hadn't Pru given me leave to call her Pru?

The idea of having a father figure in my life was unexpected. The next time I saw Mr. Dorn, we discussed the matter in some detail and I relied on the trust we had developed over the many months we had been working together to express my concerns. Trusting a male did not come easily to me, yet I had to admit I greatly enjoyed Bill Dorn's company, his brilliant mind, dry wit, and innate elegance of character.

"I'm just not at all sure I can call you, *Bill* quite honestly. And what on earth will Pru think of you taking a Tennessee country girl like me under your wing as a *daughter*?"

"Well, as far as Pru goes, it's really none of her business," he said with a firm tone. "But she asks about you and your progress on a regular basis, and both of us appreciate how much effort you are putting in to trying to better yourself." Not wanting me to misunderstand, he continued, "I'm not insulting your Appalachian heritage, Esther. You and those who have grown up here are a remarkable group of people—having learned to survive so well on so little, and having such an ingenuity about so many things. I'm just trying to add some polish, so you feel comfortable in any environment, amongst any group of people. And you're a brilliant young woman and making such wonderful progress!" He was a man who praised rarely, yet he was always sincere when positive words came.

"And what am I to call you, then?"

"At school, call me Bill, or Mr. Dorn if you prefer. Outside of school, why don't you call me Papa?"

And thus did I experience what the Psalmist says about God setting the solitary in families.

Chapter Twenty

Papa took his role of father to this daughter very much to heart. Over nearly three decades, he was a steadfast support to me in every possible way. We enjoyed many happy moments together, made all the more sweet by our mutual realization that our father-daughter bond was completely voluntary and without any obligation of DNA.

When I decided to change careers and return to school, Papa was my staunchest supporter of doing so, and he was extremely proud of me the day I graduated with a *Juris Doctor*.

At the point in his life when he was revising his will, Papa offered me his home and much of his worldly wealth. Not only did I know he also wanted to support a charity that meant a great deal to him, but, by that point in time, I had integrated Bill Dorn's value system into my own.

"No, thanks, Papa. I appreciate your generosity, but your preferred charity deserves that money." I was adamant, even about the handling of his estate. "I don't want anyone to say I was your daughter for money, Papa. Please find someone else to be your executor. I'll gladly handle any Power of Attorney for your health care, but I don't want to touch your money. Our relationship is too precious to me to have any taint put on it."

At the time of his passing in 2006, Bill Dorn had bestowed upon me a far greater legacy than any amount of wealth could provide. He had literally transformed me.

But he didn't do it alone.

Chapter Twenty-One

Parallel to the time that Papa and I began my "Pygmalion" transformation, my old pickup truck blew out transmission number three, and I was tired of all the repair bills, especially while trying to attend school and pay for Sam's upkeep. It was time for the student to become a teacher in her own right.

I rented studio space with a local music store and began advertising for beginner through early intermediate pupils. I also went to a local bank and borrowed a modest sum and went truck shopping.

My quest took me to a local Jeep dealership, Grayson Pontiac-Jeep. A very sympathetic salesman stood, incredulous, as I drove onto the lot in that beat-up, rusted-out pickup truck, with rotted oak flatbed and failing transmission.

Thanks to his kindness, I drove off the lot with a stripped, Jeep Comanche pickup. I was happily oblivious to the lack of air conditioning, the vinyl seats and flooring, and the four-in-the-floor manual transmission. I was focused on the fact that the Jeep's transmission would go in reverse without any pushing on my part, and I was deeply grateful and delighted.

Charlie, the salesman, told me as he handed me the keys, "I didn't make a dime on this deal, but I could not let you leave in that heap you drove in. I just couldn't let that happen." Bless you, Charlie.

I began to teach piano, and some of my pupils have become lifelong friends:

The Reece family, who so kindly gave Sam a home for a time when I could not afford to board him while I was in school. Tara was my very first piano student. Her sister, Amy, began her own lifelong love affair with horses thanks to her many happy moments with Sam while he was in their back yard.

The Stroud family, mom Sadie and daughter Sarah were my only "mother-daughter" student duo, and both have considerable musical talent. The "Stroud Crowd" has welcomed me to every holiday, hymn sing, and cookout, and I am grateful to count Sadie as another sister.

Speaking of adult students, I was quite surprised one day when an adult female pupil walked into the studio and asked, in an authoritative tone, "Who owns that Jeep Comanche out front?"

"I do," I responded in a muted voice, intimidated by the person who spoke.

Before me stood one of the most elegant, polished women I had ever met. She was on par with Pru Dorn, to be sure—well-dressed, well-coiffed, and extremely sophisticated in her bearing and speech. Here was a lady, beyond all doubt.

She looked me over for a moment and then extended her hand with a lovely smile. "Hello. I'm your new student, Doris Grayson."

My Friend Sam

Doris Shilliday Grayson is the daughter of two schoolteachers who raised Doris and her brother John in the Shaker Heights region of Cleveland, Ohio. Doris married her high-school sweetheart, Arthur Grayson, and they have been one another's steadfast best friend for over fifty years at this point.

When I first met Doris, it was because Mr. Grayson had decided to surprise his beloved wife with the gift of a piano. But not just any piano would do. Mr. Grayson is a brilliant, successful businessman with a kind heart toward his family, and he wanted Doris to have the best piano possible. So he called Steinway and Sons, New York, and ordered a piano. But even beyond a Steinway, Doris' piano had to be *perfect*.

So Mr. Grayson discussed the finish with Steinway and Sons, and wood samples were made so that an exact match to Doris' living room furniture would be obtained. Four months later, her custom-built Steinway arrived. What a lovely gift.

But she now had to learn to play it.

Doris and I got along extremely well as teacher and pupil. Her intelligence matches her husband's. Doris has a gentle wisdom about so many various aspects of life; it was easy for her piano teacher to absorb life lessons from Doris even as I was teaching her scales and chords and Christmas carols.

At some point, Doris decided she would prefer to have me teach her at home, on her own piano, and who could blame her? Thus began a long-term, in-home teaching arrangement that has resulted in Doris being proficient at Beethoven and Chopin, among others.

Over time, my regular visits to Doris' home provided opportunities for me to help her in various ways—an additional hand when she was pushed to get the Christmas decorating completed before a party, or feeding the beloved family cat when she and Mr. Grayson were away.

Doris represents the absolute best of charitable, elegant womanhood and she has taught me everything from how to make her mother's meatloaf to how to run a business successfully.

Doris has been like a beloved aunt or "othermother" to me for nearly thirty years. I could write an entire book filled with all the ways Doris has been my mentor and friend, yet I will write only what is already here. Doris is a very private person. She has told me more than once that what she cherishes most about our friendship is my absolute trustworthiness to maintain confidences.

What she may not realize is she, herself, has taught me that trustworthiness. She continuously inspires me to emulate her in every way, including her preference for privacy.

The point for any reader of this book to understand about Doris is, while the words may be few, her impact on my life has been, and continues to be, profound, and profoundly positive.

So Papa and Doris have been instrumental in my development as a human being—at least for any of the positives one might see in me. I take sole responsibility for any negatives as the result of the self-centeredness and impetuosity that accompanies immaturity.

Chapter Twenty-Two

I generally rode Sam in a western saddle and privately scoffed at how silly English riders look, with their tight breeches, tiny saddles, and all the bits and reins that make up a double bridle. Sam and I were so in tune with one another, I hardly needed a bit to guide him. Over time, I purchased a short-shanked, fleece-lined hackamore for Sam. This device does not include a bit, but guides the horse through applying slight pressure to the nose. The horse responds to the pressure by dropping his head, relaxing his body, and slowing down or halting. Sam loved the hackamore, and we got to the point where I rarely rode Sam with a bit anymore. The bits I had used over the years were western bits called "curb" bits, and they work by applying leverage under the horse's chin. Curb bits, used with a knowledgeable rider, can be a light and effective aid. Overly strong or harsh hands on a curb bit can damage a horse's mouth, its psyche, or both.

Fortunately, I had never been harsh in Sam's mouth with a curb bit, so he had no issues with the mechanism. Still, we both greatly preferred the hackamore and the freedom it gave Sam's mouth.

Then, one day, I happened to see a short segment of a cutting horse competition on television. I had never seen anything like that before, with the horse cutting a calf out of a small herd and then keeping the calf separated, or "cut" from the herd. The horse looked like it was dancing! He was a rich russet color, with flowing mane and tail, and he was almost on his knees as he lunged sideways or scampered a step or two, mirroring the calf's movements and preventing it from reentering the herd. Cutting looked like such fun!

I told Sam all about what I had seen and then told him, "We should learn to do that!"

I asked around and got the name of a reputable trainer and made a phone call. "How's your seat?" was the first question posed to me over the phone, and the stern, deep voice of the cowboy on the other end of the phone gave me pause.

"My seat?" I was uncertain as to what the cowboy wanted to know.

"You know, your seat? How well do you keep your butt in the saddle?" Perhaps I was mistaken, but I thought I heard a bit of annoyance creep into the cowboy's voice.

"Oh! Well, I've never come off Sam, if that's what you mean." I replied cheerily, confident in my beloved riding partner.

There was a bit of a pause, and finally the cowboy asked, "Have you ever taken any dressage lessons?"

"Dressage? You mean like, *English* lessons? Heavens, no!" I was incredulous. I rode trails with Sam and wanted to learn cutting. I had absolutely no interest in English riding, and most certainly *zero* interest in the seemingly snooty world of formal dressage.

Dressage, I knew, was a French word that means, *training*. The riding style evolved many hundreds of years ago, and it basically involves getting every component of a horse's body to respond, both independently and in specific groups, to a rider's slightest aids. The rider's aids are supposed to be her leg and seat, with only a touch of rein for guidance. Sort of like how the motor and brakes actually operate a car, and the steering wheel is only for, well, steering.

"If you want to ride a cutting horse, you've got to have a good seat. They move so quick, they'll dump you if you don't have a seat that'll stick like glue to the back of your horse, yet still allow him the freedom to move. If you want to learn cutting from me, you'll need to take two years of dressage lessons and then call me back."

"Two *years*?" I couldn't believe what I was hearing. I didn't want to take *two* dressage lessons, let alone two *years* of that type of training.

"Yep, two years," the cowboy confirmed, unconcerned about my reaction. "You find yourself a good dressage teacher and take two years of weekly lessons, and then call me back."

I hung up the phone and found myself wondering if maybe Sam and I should just stick to trail riding.

Still, over the next weeks and months, the notion that maybe my riding wasn't all it could be haunted me and made me wonder if I wasn't being fair to Sam.

I don't know if it was a situation where, "when the pupil is ready, the teacher will come" or what, exactly, but soon thereafter circumstances put Sam and me in a situation where I could watch several dressage riders training their horses. Some rode using snaffle bits, training bits with a link or "hinge" in the middle, so a rider can't exert undue pressure on the horse's mouth. I liked that idea. Other, more advanced riders rode with a full double bride, including not one but *two* bits in the horse's mouth, a snaffle and a curb, used in combination. To the uninformed, a horse working correctly in a double bridle can resemble the "set" heads of carriage horses with checkreins attached to their harness. Checkreins force a horse's head to remain at a certain level. If you've read *Black Beauty,* you've heard about checkreins from the horse's point of view. From a modern woman's perspective, try carrying sacks of groceries in your arms while wearing stilettos and hiking straight up a hill *without* leaning forward to counterbalance yourself, and you'll have some idea of the difficulties horses face when harnessed with check reins. As I studied the horses working in a double bridle, however, I began to see that, contrary to my first impression, most of these horses were not being forced to carry themselves in a compressed frame, with their chin tucked toward their chest. Rather, they had their hindquarters so completely engaged underneath them their *body* had approached their *chin*, not the other way around. The finely arched neck and vertical head carriage was a byproduct of the body being so balanced, not the result of rider cruelty in cranking the horse's face toward its body. The physics involved were totally opposite of what I had assumed. I was intrigued.

I signed us up for some basic dressage lessons, and Sam and I showed up for our first one with our western tack because it was all we had. The instructor, a patient and understanding woman named Carol, kindly loaned me her dressage saddle without saying a word about Sam's hackamore. I rode in jeans and thick-soled cowboy boots. I'm sure Sam and I made an interesting picture as we headed out to the arena on the farm where Carol taught.

Carol put us through our paces, so to speak, having me work Sam at a walk and a trot. I found the English saddle to be slippery and insecure, and more than once I felt like I was going to come right off Sam like butter slides off a hot piece of corn on the cob. Sam would raise his head during those moments, trying to rebalance himself and stay under his unexpectedly wobbly rider. I sat the trot, or tried to—Sam's trot felt incredibly strong and pointed through the few layers of leather in Carol's saddle, and I bounced hard with every step. Sam hated to gallop, so when Carol asked us for the English equivalent, "canter," Sam just trotted faster and I bounced harder. Sam and I were used to trail riding for hours at a time and coming back happily tired yet somehow refreshed. Our first dressage lesson lasted thirty minutes and by the time we headed back to the barn, Sam was soaking wet and I was utterly exhausted, with a sore backside and chafed, burning thighs.

"Your seat needs work," Carol stated the obvious. "You can use my saddle if you like, but you'll need to get an English bridle and snaffle bit. The hackamore is fine for trail riding, but you'll want to snaffle to help keep Sam's head down."

"Why do I care whether his head is down or not?" I asked. "Surely after all the years we've been riding partners Sam knows what is most comfortable for himself, doesn't he?" Carol looked at me with a patient smile. "You should care whether his head is down or not because when his head goes up it forces his back to go down. When his back is down, it means he's uncomfortable, and when he's uncomfortable, it means you're not riding correctly."

"Are you saying I am causing Sam to feel pain?" I never wanted to harm Sam. Ever.

"Not pain, exactly, but discomfort. You need to learn to ride with a more balanced body so Sam can arch his back and it can work like a spring to carry your weight most effectively. As you're learning, the snaffle will help encourage Sam to keep his body in the correct frame. You'll both be learning, and all of it will help Sam." She patted Sam's neck as we walked together. "After all," she looked at me with an earnest gaze, "in the end, it's ALL about the HORSE."

I couldn't have agreed more.

I bought a cheap, used English bridle and a brand new snaffle bit for Sam. And with fifteen years of horse ownership under my belt, at last I began to learn to ride.

Chapter Twenty-Three

At one point, Sam and I found ourselves in a rather dire financial situation. I was teaching fifty-eight private students each week and still could hardly pay all the bills. On January 1, 1998, I found myself alone and weeping, knowing I was down to two choices: find a way to make more money, or sell Sam.

Sam and I had been together for twenty-three years by then, so selling Sam was simply not an option. I sat outside alone as snow flurries fell around me, tears streaming down my cheeks, vowing with all my heart, "Don't worry, Sam. I won't sell you. *I do not sell FAMILY.*" And Sam was, in a very real sense, the only immediate family I had at the time.

As my mind grew numb from trying to work out a solution, my thoughts quieted and I heard a voice speak to me, as clearly as though another person were nearby, talking aloud.

"Go to law school. I need more Christian lawyers."

The idea of attending law school had never, ever occurred to me before. There were numerous teachers in my background, but no lawyers nor judges. My sister worked within the judicial system, but she had worked her way up by her bootstraps, as they say, and was not an attorney.

Yet the instruction was so clear I never hesitated. On January 4, when the University of Tennessee resumed operations after the Christmas break, I walked into the UT Law Admissions Office and told the very cheery lady, Caroline, at the counter, that I was there to attend law school in the autumn of that same year.

Carolyn gently informed me that applications for the entering class were already submitted, but that I could gather all the information and submit it for the following year, 1999.

"But I'm supposed to start *this* fall, ma'am." I stood steadfast, convinced I was being divinely guided.

"Well, there's one final opportunity to take the L.S.A.T. in early February," Carolyn offered, "but most students study for months before taking it."

"What's the L.S.A.T.?"

"Well," Carolyn, ever the accomplished professional, maintained her composure, even when faced with such abject ignorance about the law school entrance process, "it's an entrance exam. You have to take the test and achieve a certain score as one of the criteria for entrance into the law school."

She very helpfully gave me an application packet and I went to the UT Bookstore, where I found, and purchased, a slim paperback book entitled *Thirty Days to the L.S.A.T.*

I had twenty-eight days, so I doubled up on some days of the self-guided study course, so I would complete the book the night before the February L.S.A.T.

Chapter Twenty-Four

"Well, Sam, tomorrow's the big day," I worked the tangles out of his mane and tail with my fingers, opting to groom him without brushes. Just touching Sam, hearing him munch his hay in the quiet evening, made me feel less nervous. He raised his head from the pile of hay on his stall floor and turned a dark brown eye in my direction.

"Thanks for the vote of confidence, my friend. If I can do well, get into law school, and get a good job, we won't ever have to worry about money, ever again, Sam. Somehow, God is going to make this happen, I can just *feel* it!"

The next morning, a Saturday, dawned bright and clear. It was February, and I was grateful for the lack of snow that day. I didn't know a single soul in the room during the L.S.A.T.

During scheduled breaks between sections of the test, while other test-takers gathered in groups—obviously they were friends who were planning to attend law school *en mass*—I went outside and sat quietly, reviewing notes in my mind and praying for clarity of thought and comprehensive memory. I approached the L.S.A.T. the same way Papa had taught me to play a piano recital.

During a piano recital, each piece was one component of an entire tapestry of sound for the evening, however, the wise pianist focused on each piece one at a time during the actual performance. The opening Baroque work, once played, could not assist one in an accurate and artistic execution of the following Classical piece.

Papa's point was multi-fold, and very smart. If I started a recital with a Bach fugue, and it went well, allowing myself the luxury of pleasure, or the mental let-down of relief, did absolutely nothing but distract from the upcoming Beethoven sonata. Likewise, if the fugue had fallen to pieces, allowing the mental demons from that failure to wreak havoc with the sonata was self-defeating.

The only way to really survive a piano recital was to focus on the piece at hand and, once the last note sounded, set it aside mentally as though it never existed, and focus on the next piece. Debriefing and lessons learned could occur the following day, or whenever, but in the middle of a recital, the only piece that matters is the one you're about to play.

In similar fashion, I took the L.S.A.T. one section at a time, and, while I heard the voices of others agonizing about, "What did you put for question twenty-five" or whatever, I was blissfully insulated from any self-doubt throughout the test by following Papa's sage advice and setting aside the prior set of questions to clear my mind for what was to come.

In such a manner, by the end of the day, I was mentally fatigued but feeling rather positive about the entire L.S.A.T. experience. While I had no idea if I had scored well or not, I knew I had done my best, and I told Sam so that evening.

"It was a hard test, Sam, but not impossibly so." The soft glow of his stall light added cheer to the crisp winter night air. "I've got two references, both from lawyers whose children or grandchildren I have taught piano, so now I need to write an essay. But what, Sam, shall I write about?" I sat on an overturned bucket in the corner of his stall and pondered about my choice of topics, while Sam positioned himself so I could scratch his favorite spots, first one side, then the other.

Once, in high school, I had written an informational essay on hoof laminitis. While I had received an "A" on the paper, my decidedly *un*horsey English teacher, Mrs. Thompson, had forbidden me to write on equine ailments in any future assignments.

While Mrs. Thompson would not be grading my law school entrance essay, I decided writing about anything horsey might not be a good idea. "Sorry, Sam. I think I'd best write about something besides horses this time."

He turned toward me to get his ears scratched as I sat there, thinking. "Besides, buddy, if I started writing about you, I doubt I could keep it within the word limit!" He snorted softly and then stuck his tongue into my hand, and we played tongue-game while I kept thinking.

At one point in undergraduate school, I had taken a job at a local deli. The deli served breakfast, as well as lunch and dinner, and there was an elegant African-American lady, Lela, who was the deli's biscuit maker.

Lela was a very large lady and ponderous of movement, and most folks would probably look at her and think she was slow of mind, as well. Lela, however, was very quick-witted. She was also savvy enough to be slow to speak, which meant she heard a great deal and gossiped not at all. Lela taught me to make biscuits. More importantly, her biscuit-making skills taught me about how to handle people, which is, oddly enough, the same way I had learned to handle horses: gently, carefully, and at whatever pace was best for the horse, or the person.

Or the biscuit.

Lela's massive hands would empty five-pound sacks of flour into an enormous bowl. She would quasi-measure baking powder and salt, shortening and buttermilk into the flour, using her instincts just as much as any measuring cup or spoon. Next, she would take a pastry cutter and blend the mix. It seemed to take forever; she worked so slowly and carefully. The secret, Lela taught me, was to never let your skin touch the biscuit dough unless absolutely necessary. So Lela used the pastry cutter until the mix was thoroughly blended. Then she gently turned the huge wad of dough onto a well-floured wooden board. Her touch seemed featherlight as she pushed the dough out toward the edges of the board until it was less than an inch thick. Then she took a biscuit cutter, dipped it in loose flour, and cut the dough with a surgeon's precision. Lela's biscuits were the lightest I had ever tasted. Still are. But the point is, I chose to write about Lela and her biscuit making for my law school essay.

I knew no judges, and very few lawyers, and absolutely nothing about being a lawyer. But one thing I did know: people need help, and, in order to help them, one must communicate effectively, kindly, and gently. Lela had taught me that, and I felt like it was worth writing about.

A few hours later, as I read the final draft to Sam, I commented, "Well, Sam, even if this doesn't help me get into law school, it is a tribute to a wonderful but unknown lady named Lela, and she deserves to have folks know who she is. Including some intellectuals like law professors."

With the L.S.A.T. behind me, and all my application paperwork submitted, there was nothing left for me to do but wait.

I kept teaching piano students, kept buying Sam's feed, and kept watching my own pantry dwindle down to nothing more than soup and crackers. Still, though, I never missed a meal, or a mortgage payment, and I was grateful that somehow, like that widow in the Bible with the bit of meal in the bottom of the barrel, there was always one more can of soup in the pantry, each and every time I looked for food.

In mid-March 1998, I received an envelope from the University of Tennessee College of Law. Inside the envelope was a single sheet of paper. That piece of paper changed my life forever.

"Welcome to the University of Tennessee College of Law."

"Sam! We're in! We're in! We made it! We're going to law school, Sam!

Chapter Twenty-Five

Apparently my law school application did something right, because UT also very kindly provided me with a scholarship for my 1L year. I had no idea what 1L meant at the time, as I'd never watched *The Paper Chase*—or any law-related movie.

"You know, Sam," I chatted with him from atop his back as we enjoyed a ride together the next day, "I think I should probably go visit a court or something, don't you think?" Since most of my piano students came for lessons after school, my days were somewhat free, so I decided to venture downtown to the City County Building the next day and see what I could learn about my new profession.

It was a Thursday, and there was a great deal of activity outside the Fourth Circuit Court, so I slipped inside and sat down. The courtroom was outfitted with light oak wood, not the typical dark cherry or walnut I had expected. The Judge was presenting a slide presentation, which included a circle diagram, divided into three portions.

"The circle of domestic violence always occurs in three phases," he instructed to all present. I squinted to make out his name, which was etched into the aged brass nameplate high upon the bench. Judge Swann.

His Honor continued, "First, there's a 'honeymoon phase,' where everything seems good. Then, tension begins to build. When the tension gets great enough, an act occurs. Sometimes it is merely yelling. Sometimes it involves physical violence. Typically, the perpetrator soon feels remorse and asks forgiveness, and the victim forgives them. They go through another honeymoon phase, and the cycle begins again."

I watched as one person after another stood in front of the podium and spoke with the judge. Sitting in the jury box were about a dozen men, all wearing black and white striped jumpsuits, and all chained together, hand and foot, so none could move without all of them moving. Armed guards stood on either end of the jury box. It was a compelling scene.

After a couple of hours, the judge called a uniformed gentleman with snow-white hair to the bench. They spoke quietly, and the next thing I knew, the uniformed gentleman opened up the swinging partition between where the judge's bench was and the rest of the courtroom. He walked down the aisle between the rows of spectator benches, and, to my surprise, he stopped beside me. Instantly, I was terrified, wondering what I had done to draw attention to me. All I had wanted to do was sit and observe and learn as much as I could during the months before I started law school.

"What is your name, and why are you here, miss?" His face, while kind, was firm, as was his voice.

I told him my name and said, "I just found out I got into law school, sir, and so I thought I should come down here and observe some court activity and learn whatever I can

My Friend Sam

about how the legal system works before I start school in the autumn."

The uniformed gentleman seemed shocked by my response. He turned to Judge Swann with a look of incredulity on his face.

"Your Honor?"

"Yes, Mr. Bailiff."

"The lady says she is gonna be a 1L at UT this fall, and she's here to observe and learn!" I was mystified by the tone of his voice, and even more so when the judge responded, "What? Are you serious?"

The bailiff looked at me, as if daring me to change my story. I met his scrutiny without flinching, knowing I had told the absolute truth.

"She's not lying, Judge."

Judge Swann stood up and spoke directly to me. "Come here, miss." I obediently followed the bailiff, crossing what I later learned was "the bar"—that swinging low wooden door—for the very first time.

"In all my years as a judge, miss, I don't ever recall a student coming down here to learn about courts prior to actually being enrolled in school, either for a class or some other assignment."

"I've been a musician, sir, and don't know the first thing about being an attorney." Perhaps it was my candor about my own ignorance that impressed His Honor, but, for whatever reason, he then said:

"Thursday is always Order of Protection day on my docket. We're always overloaded, and you can not only learn a great deal, you can help!"

With that, he gave me instructions to sit at Counsel Table for the remainder of the day, and then learn about client interviewing and intake from the court clerk staff.

Esther L. Roberts

Every Thursday from April until August 1998, I spent at Fourth Circuit, helping abused women fill out the requisite paperwork to file for orders of protection against the men who had abused them. The work was instructive in every possible way, and I remain extremely grateful to Judge Swann for his kindness in allowing this incoming law student to learn so much from His Honor and his excellent staff.

Chapter Twenty-Six

In order to save money, I asked some dear friends, David and Sadie Stroud, to help me build Sam a small lean-to behind my little house in a neighborhood in west Knoxville. I'm almost certain it was against the law to have livestock in my back yard. But Sam was like a big dog, only he never barked, and I was desperate to save money while attending law school.

Law students, particularly first year students, are not supposed to work at all, but I had to keep teaching piano in order to pay my bills, so I shifted my teaching schedule to accommodate my class schedule, and never told the law school administration I was still teaching while in school.

I loved having Sam right there. I could study in the backyard and he would be right with me. The yard had a six-foot wooden privacy fence, so nobody could see Sam, except when I took him out. I knew I had to carefully manage his manure, so I scooped it up and put it in black lawn/leaf trash bags and put it in the trash bin for the trash service to haul off. I paid for the service, so I didn't feel guilty about that, other than the fact that I'm sure my trash bin was always one of the heaviest on my street, as it was always filled to the brim with bags full of horse apples.

I took Sam for a walk almost every day to make sure he got some exercise despite his cramped quarters, and I'm sure we made quite a sight, walking on the sidewalk alongside a busy four-lane road. We generally walked about three miles, round trip, and, on the weekends, I would trailer Sam to a nearby park and go riding.

Lakeshore Park is a lovely place, with miles of walking/jogging trails, open spaces for lively games of Frisbee or touch football, and several baseball and sports fields for organized team sports in Knoxville. Many people walk their dogs there. To my knowledge, I'm the only person who ever brought a horse there. But Sam and I went there on a fairly regular basis during my law school years. I had a two-horse trailer by this time, and I would haul him over to the park for an afternoon of riding, grazing, and relaxing. Sam enjoyed these outings, as he loved meeting new people, and we always drew a crowd.

These moments with Sam were precious, because the rest of the time I was either studying or teaching. For this creative soul, the first semester of law school was a shocking and difficult transition.

In the world of music, there is great respect given to one's professors, and they are, "professor so-and-so" during class. After class, however, professors and students often work together on preparing the same musical number together, be it an opera, musical, band concert, etc.

So, in music, things get decidedly less formal outside of class, and many times everyone ends up on a first-name basis. While there are egos aplenty, and divas galore, still, the artistic community in general understands that creativity thrives in a less formal environment. Innovation is encouraged and the questioning of authority is not considered *prima facie* disrespectful. The instructive process is one of iterative gleaning and learning by example.

The world of law, by contrast, demands formality, order, structure, and, insofar as is humanly possible, a reasonably predictable outcome. The Socratic method—teaching by demanding the student discern the answer to a sometimes obtuse question—was completely foreign to me, as was being steadfastly addressed by my surname.

There seemed to be a palpable barrier between me and my professors, as well as between me and my fellow students. The students ran the gamut—some were descended from a long line of lawyers and judges; others, like me, had no lawyers in their family tree whatsoever.

I was not always eloquent in class. At least once, I was so impetuous as to garner the ridicule of both my torts professor and the entire class, much to my humiliation and shame. Upon reflection, the ridicule was warranted, but that didn't make it any easier to bear in the moment.

Over time, I found my stride, so to speak, in law school. And Sam was with me every step of the way. Through law review, having my case note published, working as research assistant to the eminent legal scholar, Professor Joseph Cook, Sam was there.

Sam was there even when we spent my 2L summer in Oklahoma City, as the student law clerk to Oklahoma Supreme Court Chief Justice Hardy Summers.

Chapter Twenty-Seven

During autumn break of my 1L year, I packed up my one good suit and a stack of resumes and headed to Oklahoma. I had this idea that, upon graduating law school, I would move to Oklahoma City and practice law out west.

Oklahoma City is home to some of the largest horse shows in the world and, despite the fact that Sam and I didn't show very often, I thought Oklahoma would be a good, horse-friendly place for a fresh start.

The state Capitol of Oklahoma was constructed to house all three branches of the state's government. The building is massive and elegant, filled with black-veined white Vermont marble columns and stairways, and lots of large windows inside the building to make it very bright and transparent. It is several stories high, with a rotunda on each floor that showcases original artwork—large canvases that reflect various aspects of Oklahoma's history, from the Native American populace (from which the state's name is derived, *Okla* meaning *red* and *homa* meaning *human*) to the oil boom. My favorite painting was a group of five ballerinas, all of whom are Native American and world-class dancers.

The governor and deputy governor were housed in one corridor of the Capitol building; the legislature's offices were spread out over several floors, and the appellate courts, including the Court of Criminal Appeals and the Supreme Court of the State of Oklahoma, were housed on the second floor.

I didn't know a soul in the legal community of Oklahoma, but I walked up the Capitol steps, stack of resumes in hand, determined to ask anyone I met if there were any summer internships available for out-of-state students like me.

I spent the morning going from office to office, and everyone was cordial, but no one seemed to have any openings. I paused at the rotunda on each level, admiring the artwork and wondering how I could ever hope to get a job there. Oklahoma had three law schools within the state at that time, which meant there were three 1Ls who ranked #1 in each of their respective classes. Surely a native Oklahoman who was first in his or her respective law class would have already snagged the best internships available, especially over a completely unknown Tennessean who was not #1 in her class. But I keep pressing on, hoping to talk with someone and perhaps find some type of work, even as a legislative page, for the summer.

Heavy glass doors protected the entryway into the Supreme Court wing of the Capitol building, and I felt an almost overwhelming sense of quiet dignity as I walked down the silent hallway. Large suites on each side of the hall comprised the justices' chambers. Wherever a dark, massive door stood open I could see a legal secretary sitting at her desk, surrounded by law books and a computer.

The Chief Justice's chambers were at the end of the hallway. There, a receptionist screened everyone, even the

My Friend Sam

Justice's legal secretary from unsolicited contact with outsiders.

I stopped by each suite and asked to submit my resume. My request was met with the same polite variation of, "We'll be happy to give this to His (or Her) Honor, but judicial clerkships fill up fairly quickly, etc., etc."

At last, out of resumes and with my hopes fading, I turned to retrace my steps and leave the Supreme Court wing of the building. As I walked, it occurred to me I had yet to see the actual Supreme Court courtroom, and I pondered wandering around to take a quick look before I left the building. Lost in my thoughts, I didn't hear the footsteps behind me until I was approaching the heavy glass doors and pushed them open to leave the Supreme Court wing. Noting someone was almost directly behind me, I paused and held open the door.

"Thank you."

I glanced at the gentleman behind me and noted his white hair and tall, elegant bearing as I said, "You're welcome." I started to walk on, but paused as he spoke again. "You're not a familiar face." It was more a query than a statement, and I wondered if he was plainclothes security for the Justices.

"No sir, I'm not from here. I'm a law student from Tennessee, looking for work next summer."

"Tennessee?" He seemed surprised. "That's quite a ways away."

"Nearly 900 miles, sir, but I really want to work in Oklahoma, and so I came out here and," I paused as a bit of embarrassed self-consciousness swept over me, "I've been handing out resumes all morning, trying to find work."

"You came here, to the State Capitol, to find a summer job?" His eyes were calm and steady but his voice betrayed his incredulity.

I could only imagine how ridiculous I must seem to this stranger. The full force of my audacity struck me in that moment, and I could only reply with a quiet, "Yes, sir."

"Why?" The shortness of his query certainly didn't mask the multidimensional curiosity underlying it. I could almost read his mind in that moment. *Why would anyone out of state presume they could just walk into another state's Capitol and literally take a coveted judicial clerkship away from a native son or daughter? Who would be so incredibly naïve? So stupid?*

I looked directly at him for a moment and decided to be completely candid. After all, if he were security, he certainly didn't appear in a hurry to have me escorted off the premises, and he was a kind gentleman. He also seemed genuinely intrigued.

"Because I really want to move to Oklahoma once I've graduated law school, sir. I don't know anyone in the legal community here—"

He interrupted and no longer attempted to mask his surprise. "You don't know a *soul*? Not one single person?"

"Not in the legal community, sir. I have a couple of friends who live here, but they have no legal connections, either. So, I thought what have I got to lose except a couple of days and the price of the trip out here?" I paused, but he waited for me to continue. "So I came out here and I've distributed copies of my resume to anyone who would take one. But I know the chances are slim to none. Oklahoma has three law schools and each of them has a 1L who is tops in their class right now. I'm not #1 in my class, although my grades are good and I am a diligent student."

My Friend Sam

"Who also has an extraordinary bit of gumption, I might add," he said with a kind smile.

"Thank you, sir."

"So, where are you headed right now, Miss, *ah*?" he let the question linger.

"Roberts, sir. I'm Esther Roberts."

"And where are you headed right now, Ms. Roberts?"

"Well, I was about to leave the building, but I would love to see the Supreme Court courtroom before I go." I turned my head and peered back down the hallway. "I'm just not sure where it is, to be honest."

He smiled with one of those genuine smiles that light up a person's whole face. "Come with me; I'll show you."

"Thank you very much!" I replied enthusiastically, and followed him down another corridor that ended with two massive wooden doors. He opened the doors and we entered one of the most spectacular rooms I have ever seen. The courtroom was so beautiful, my eyes took it in as a collage of architecture: Huge columns of white Vermont marble; a rich, wooden judicial bench with an ornately carved header and separate, velvet-lined entryways for each Justice; large, multi-paned windows where the bright Oklahoma sunlight flooded the room; aged benches to accommodate the audience; massive wooden counsel desks and equally massive chairs. The color scheme was various shades of green, accented with light peach and white trim. The ceiling was strikingly similar to the recessed, ornate, rosette style of the United States Supreme Court courtroom. I was awestruck into silence by the stunning beauty of the room. My benevolent tour guide stood at the front of the room and watched me as I meandered slowly about the room, taking it all in. He partially blocked a lovely portrait of the current Justices, but there was so much else to look at, I hardly noticed. He began to chat about various aspects of the courtroom.

"Oklahoma became a state in 1907. Our Capitol wasn't built until some years after that, including after the United States Supreme Court courtroom had been constructed. Because of that, the early Oklahoma Supreme Court decided to utilize the U.S. Supreme Court courtroom as a guide of sorts."

"So that explains the similarity of the ceiling design."

"Indeed." He eyed me as carefully as I studied the room around us. "Tell me more about yourself, Ms. Roberts."

I gave him some details regarding my background, including my varied background in the sciences and music, and my initial career as a musician.

"So why are you going to law school?" His question was direct and the probative tone of his voice made me wonder again if perhaps he might be Capitol security.

"For a couple of reasons, actually. First of all, God has blessed me with a good, strong mind and I want to utilize that gift in the best way possible. Adjusting to law school has been challenging, but I am convinced I will develop into a good attorney, and I would like to live and work in Oklahoma someday. A summer internship will help me learn specific points of Oklahoma law, and also, hopefully help me make contacts for future jobs. The other reason is this: being a professional musician in Tennessee is a wonderful thing, but it also means there are many, many talented musicians around my area of the country, being so close to Nashville and all, and it's hard to make a decent living unless you are truly gifted. I'm a good pianist, but not a truly *great* one, so there won't be any recording deals in my future."

My Friend Sam

We both chuckled and then I continued, "I have a horse—Sam—whom I've had since I was a young girl. He is my very best friend, odd as that may sound. But I want to be able to provide a good home for Sam and never have to worry about whether I can buy feed for him or whatever. Becoming an attorney will hopefully allow me to achieve that objective. Maybe it sounds bad that part of the reason I am going to law school is for economic stability, but I have a responsibility to Sam and I have no intention of shirking that responsibility."

Given my feelings for Sam, my voice had risen with intensity as I spoke, and the last phrase, "I have no intention of shirking that responsibility" seemed to ring in the air and echo around us in the silence that followed. I was totally embarrassed by this. I took a deep breath and steeled myself for the outburst of laughter that would surely follow.

Surprisingly, none came.

Instead, my tour guide studied me silently for a moment, and then began closing the distance between us. I was so focused on his approach that I failed to realize the portrait of the Justices was now in full view.

The tall, white-haired gentleman stopped in front of me, looked down at me with a cordial smile, and extended his hand.

"I'm Chief Justice Hardy Summers," he said, as he shook my hand. "Your initiative is extremely impressive, coming all this way to find a job, despite not knowing a soul, and staying so true to your own values. I'd like you to be my summer intern. I'll have the paperwork drawn up and sent to you." He paused and grinned at the stunned look on my face, and then he said, "Welcome to Oklahoma."

Chapter Twenty-Eight

By the time I began my second year of law school, I wanted to give Sam more room because I just did not have time for our daily walks.

So I boarded Sam at a lovely facility in East Knox County called Crosstie Stables. At the time, Crosstie was managed by the Moir family. Crosstie sits on two sides of Mine Road, off Rutledge Pike, and features sprawling, lush acres, rolling wooded hills, and a stream so pristine beavers call it home and raise their young there. Crosstie was my sanctuary, for many reasons.

In the first place, Sam lived there. His stall was the last one on the outside row of the big white barn. From his stall, Sam could look out into the woods, or over one of the main pastures. A large overhang kept the sun at bay, and Sam's stall was always clean and cool. He was turned out every day to graze or nap or stroll to the creek. Every time I went to Crosstie, if Sam was out in the field, he came to the fence and whickered, then waited for me to grab his halter and lead rope and come get him. We enjoyed many leisurely hours, just the two of us, at Crosstie.

Another reason Crosstie was so special is because the Moirs always made me feel like family. They neither revered nor reviled me for choosing to become an attorney. To Libbi, George, and their grown children, Stacy and John, I was simply a girl with a horse and a pickup truck, like so many other clients who boarded there. I was welcome to come and ride Sam anytime, and never speak, or, if I felt like it, I was welcome to hang around and share takeout from one of the local restaurants.

During hay season, all help was welcome, and some of my best memories at Crosstie are of helping load hay on the conveyor to lift it up into the huge loft of the big white barn. One season I even got to drive John's big diesel pickup during a field gathering of hay. My job was to put the truck in low gear and then allow it to creep along, pulling a huge hay wagon, being careful to keep it straight between the rows of freshly bailed hay and not run over any of the men tossing the heavy bales onto the trailer. I also had to swing the entire rig in very large turns as we progressed around the field, to make certain none of the stacked hay shifted and fell off the wagon. I felt honored to be included among the men as they worked, and I learned just how hard farmers work to make their living.

Crosstie encompassed about 200 acres of fenced and cross-fenced fields and typically held about fifty horses, forty boarders like Sam, and ten or so of the Moir's horses. That many acres and that many horses meant fence always needed mending, and I enjoyed many a weekend fencing with the men. It was a great distraction from the mental rigors of law school.

We would start out early in the morning, before the heat of the day, and what a sight we made! Up to half a dozen pickup trucks, bouncing across the fields and through the woods, the bed of each truck filled with toolboxes full of hammers, pliers, nails and staples, rolls of wire, heavy wooden posts, bundles of metal posts, and huge coolers filled with water. I loved climbing in the cab of my own pickup and joining the convoy. And one day something wonderful happened at the end of one of these long, hard, hot fencing days.

We had all returned back to the big white barn, and the men were sitting around, cooling off and talking over the day. I had wandered off to get Sam, thinking I'd take him out and let him pick grass around the edge of the barn—a four-legged weed eater, as it were. Unbeknownst to the men, I was just out of sight, but not out of earshot, when I overheard one of them say, "That Esther, now, she's a regular hand." Among horse folk, a 'regular hand' means that person can handle just about any task given to them with respect to livestock, ranch work, and all the myriad jobs that come with life on a farm. A quiet chorus of agreement followed, along with some harmless and humorous comments about how, "It's a shame she's gonna be a lawyer . . ." "Yea, but some guy's gonna snag himself a cush life with that girl once she graduates!"

Of all the degrees, honors, and accolades I have been blessed to receive in my life, having some East Tennessee "good ol' boys" call me a "regular hand" is one of the finest compliments I have ever received.

I always felt welcome at Crosstie, and I cherished knowing I could be myself there. My *real* self. Not the law student. Not the pianist. Not even Bill Dorn's daughter. I was just a girl with a horse and a pickup truck, and to my last breath on this earth, that's really all I am, all I ever dreamed of, and all I ever wanted to be.

There was a small, add-on stall behind Sam's stall at the big white barn. The little stall was where Anna Rachel got stalled each night. "Rachel" was an aged, flea-bitten grey mare. She looked like God had taken a white horse and speckled her with black hairs all over her body. Rachel was rather small, maybe fourteen hands tall. One could tell that, earlier in her life, Rachel had been quite a fine-looking animal. Her Arabian heritage was evident in the wide forehead, large black eyes, and finely dished profile that ended in a delicate muzzle that could have, quite literally, fit into a teacup. Her intelligent eyes were kind and wise, and she was a good, quiet neighbor to Sam.

Prior to arriving at Crosstie, Rachel had been boarded in North Carolina and gossip around the barn was that she had been unintentionally bred by a rogue mustang who had jumped the fence to get to Rachel. It was rumored that Rachel was descended from Basq himself, a champion Arabian stallion and the hallmark of his breed. If a Basq daughter had been fouled by a rogue, the foal to come was destined to be a genetic waste bin, literally ill conceived, and it would undoubtedly be unwanted and despised.

On June 23, 1999, during the night, Anna Rachel, proud granddaughter of the noble Basq, gave birth in the little stall behind Sam.

Chapter Twenty-Nine

"A filly." I overheard boarders talking as I climbed out of my truck to go visit Sam. "Black." "Such a shame."

Sam was in his stall to avoid the summer heat. Crosstie, like most boarding facilities, provides night turnout during the summer and day turnout during the winter.

"Well, Sam, I hear you've got a new neighbor." Sam nudged me, asked for scratches of his favorite itchy spots, completely unconcerned about the new arrival. I peered over the stall wall and caught a glimpse of Rachel and her baby.

True to form, Rachel's pure Arabian blood had passed down many of her fine qualities to the little filly, although the filly had a heaviness of bone to her frame that was not evident in her blue-blooded mother. "She will be bigger than her mother, that's for sure, Sam." I analyzed the filly while I absently rubbed Sam. "Blaze face and three white feet." The filly was up and moving around in the stall, already in control of her gangly frame and those long, long legs. I caught a glimpse of her eye and saw a wild, unbroken spirit there. Surely her father was, indeed, a rogue mustang.

"She's going to be a handful, Sam, mark my words!" I turned to my own beloved pet and studied him for a moment. Sam's eyes were liquid brown, kind and gentle, full of quiet love and affection. "I'm so glad I have YOU!" I hugged him, put his halter on, and off we went to tack up and take a ride.

Law school is an all-consuming endeavor. Some of the wisest advice I was given upon being accepted to law school was to, "Warn your friends and family that law school will *own* you for the next three years." It is true. Between my studies, law review, clerking at a law firm and maintaining a piano studio of forty-plus students each week, my life was extremely full, and I sometimes only saw Sam on the weekends. I treasured each visit to Crosstie during law school, and my time with Sam was what kept me relaxed and focused throughout those three years. There was no time to think of Rachel and her filly, so I paid no attention when the filly was weaned. I didn't realize she was never named, and, due to her lineage, was unlikely to ever be sold. She did not get a stall in the big white barn. I had no idea what became of her, but I knew she remained at Crosstie, because once, several months later, as Sam and I were riding back to the barn after a leisurely trail ride, we came across a scene I shall never forget.

Several folks were standing around the round pen, and there was a lot of banging and clanging going on, so I turned Sam and headed over to see what was happening. When we got close enough, I saw John "flagging" a young horse. A young black horse. Or perhaps I should say, a black whirlwind. Like the Tasmanian devil of Bugs Bunny fame.

John Moir was, and is, an outstanding horseman. He has gentled many horses, including some wild mustangs, using "natural horseman" methods. One component of "natural horsemanship" is to utilize a flag on the end of a hand-held pole to help desensitize a nervous horse, help the horse focus, and, most importantly, help the horse focus on the human who is training the horse.

A horse-rider partnership, from the horse's perspective, is simply a "herd" of two—the horse and the rider. Horses, being prey animals in the wild, know two forms of self-preservation: fight and flight. "Alpha" horses will fight what scares them. Non-alpha horses will flee when frightened.

When dealing with the horse-human herd of two that comprises a riding duo, it is critical that the human be the *alpha*. The horse must trust their rider so implicitly that, regardless of whatever may arise that scares the horse, both the fight instinct and flight instinct are kept in check and the horse obeys the rider's commands through trust, not fear. This is the essence of natural horsemanship. To gain a horse's trust takes as long as it takes. It all depends on the horse. For some horses, particularly non-alpha horses, it may be a matter of moments or days. For an alpha, yielding to trust can take a very long time.

That evening, at Crosstie, everyone was spellbound by the black filly in the round pen and John's patience as he flagged her to try and get her to move around the round pen at his command. The black filly, Rachel's daughter, who was now almost a yearling, was having absolutely none of it. She flew around the round pen with her head high in the air, her nose pointed outside the round pen, doing everything she could to climb the walls of the pen and get away from that hated flag. There was no fear in her eyes, only determination. It was almost as if she could communicate—*No one will ever tame me! No one!* Round and round she flew, her hooves flint hard on the ground, her young legs strong and straight, pounding the earth with a fierceness that could not be denied. Her mane and tail streamed out as she galloped and bucked and pranced, with no trace of Rachel's sweet temperament evident in the tornado that was her offspring.

I sat in the saddle on calm, dozing Sam, and wondered why anyone would ever even attempt to handle a horse like Rachel's daughter. Surely she would kill someone before she would ever yield. Finally, realizing how tense I was even watching such a horse, I turned Sam away and headed to the barn, whispering a prayer of gratitude for my own beloved Sam.

Chapter Thirty

Sam's mother was a registered American Indian Horse. His father was a registered American Quarter Horse, of the "old school" body type. Instead of the massive, almost bodybuilder muscling of today's modern Quarter Horse, Sam's father, Tonto's Sam, was smaller and leaner, with some infusion of Thoroughbred along the way. Tonto's Sam was bred to be a racing Quarter Horse, but never made a big name for himself.

Kickapoo, Sam's mother, was built like a classic mustang, compact, tough, hardy, rather coarse and unrefined. She was a tri-color paint, basically a bay horse God had liberally splashed with white paint.

Other than his somewhat wedge-shaped head, Sam took most of his body characteristics from his mother. And that meant Sam was absolutely, positively *not* built for dressage. Horses carry roughly seventy percent of their body weight on their forelegs. Dressage trains a horse to shift their weight and carry it on their rear legs, to lighten the forehand of the horse and allow the horse to move more freely. The typical dressage horse is rather tall, with lovely long limbs that sweep through the air with fluid freedom at the walk, the trot, and the canter. The best dressage horses seem to float through the air, so elastic and springy are their movements.

Sam was neither tall, nor long of limb. His walk was supple and covered ground, at least, as much ground as a small horse could cover with each stride. His trot, far from fluid, was a teeth-jarring, choppy, disjointed gait, and, like most mustangs, Sam traveled with his head held high, always looking for the unseen predator. In sum, Sam was as much the antithesis of the standard dressage horse as I was the standard dressage rider. In similar fashion to the ideal horse, the ideal rider is tall, slim, long of leg, and extremely graceful. I am five-foot-two; tall and long of leg are just not possible in this rider.

So why on earth did I decide to enter Sam in a local dressage show? Truly, I have no idea. I guess it seemed like a good idea at the time, but I knew absolutely nothing about dressage and how it is judged. I had seen a flyer in a local tack shop, and decided my wonderful Sam was just as worthy as any other horse, so why not?

Some dear friends, the Reece family, had come to see Sam's show debut. They had very kindly allowed me to keep Sam at their farm at a point in time when I had no money to board him and no place of my own, while I was still a struggling musician and not a lawyer-to-be. The Reeces cared deeply for me, and they *loved* Sam. It was a big day for all of us. There were six horses in Sam's class, an introductory class for those horse/rider teams just beginning their study of dressage. Surely Sam had as good a chance as any other horse.

I should have doubted the wisdom of entering the show as soon as we arrived. I hauled Sam in our humble, two-horse trailer. Arriving at the show venue, we turned up a manicured drive, paralleled on both sides by stately white board fencing, and parked near a big barn that gleamed with fresh red paint. There were several exhibitors already there, and the parking lot was crowded with large trucks and elegant, expensive multi-horse trailers. Among the exhibitors, I didn't know a soul.

I glanced around as other riders off-loaded their horses. Large, elegant bays and greys backed down trailer ramps, some of them requiring two handlers to control one horse. They were cloaked in expensive blankets and had thick, blindingly white leg wraps on each leg to protect fragile bones from mishaps as the high-strung show animals traveled. I would later learn that some horses are kept "bandaged" every moment of their life except when they are competing in the show ring or being groomed. As each expensive equine was off-loaded, they were carefully inspected for damage in transit. As each one passed their owner's inspection, they were led away to spend the day sequestered in a "guest" stall, with padded walls and deep shavings cushioning the stall floor, until it was their time to compete.

Sam appeared small and humble, even to me, as I took his plain leather halter and economy cotton lead rope and backed him, unblanketed and unbandaged, off our trailer. I had no money to rent him a "guest" stall, so I tied him to the side of the trailer and hung a hay net and a water bucket within his reach. I had washed him before we came, but somehow, his white didn't seem as shiny as the light grey horses I'd been watching. I started brushing him all over again, wanting to make sure I had done everything I could to show Sam at his best, beautiful self.

Groups of slender, leggy, wealthy girls and women milled about the showgrounds, and I could hear snippets of conversation as humanity ebbed and flowed around—

refined female voices calling to one another and renewing their acquaintance; intense conversations between trainers and grooms, trainers and riders, trainers and trainers; condescending evaluations of horses.

Including Sam.

A group of girls stood nearby around a pristine truck and trailer. They were about my age, but that was all we had in common. Perhaps they thought they were out of earshot. Perhaps they didn't care.

"Who would be so stupid as to bring a *paint* horse to a dressage show?" "Well, just look at her trailer—so tiny! Obviously a nobody, with a humble little nobody of a horse, to boot." "Good news, though! One less for us to worry about!" Laughter burned my ears as the girls turned on their custom-boot heels and walked away.

"It's okay, Sam. You're just as good as any of those big horses. Don't you worry, okay?" Sam was contentedly munching hay, oblivious to any slurs from strangers. I looked down at the ground, noting my rather worn breeches. I had found them in the "pre-owned" bin at a local tack shop. My paddock boots gleamed with fresh polish, but they were not the standard, tall riding boots seen in dressage. As this was a schooling show, tall boots were not required, but I realized most riders were wearing tall boots anyway. Per the dress code on the entry form, I was wearing a white shirt with a collar, yet, when I looked around, most of the riders were in full dressage attire, including neatly tied stock and dark blue wool riding jacket. I didn't own a jacket. I had no tall boots. And Sam was the only paint horse within miles.

As the show got underway, I was surprised to hear voices calling to the riders during their test. "I'll be right back, Sam," and I walked over to the show ring to see what was going on.

My Friend Sam

Dressage is a sport of precision. Each placement of each hoof is graded, as well as the overall form of the horse, his temperament, and his movement. Dressage is divided into levels, similar to grades in school. Each level has certain movements required of the horse, and the movements increase in difficulty as one moves up the levels, from "introductory" to "Grand Prix."

Each level is subdivided into "tests" and, during a dressage show, every horse and rider pair exhibits a particular "test" to at least one judge. Each test is comprised of elements, including circles, diagonal lines, serpentine patterns, changes of gait from walk to trot, trot to canter, etc. Each element is scored from 0 (not executed) to 10 (perfect). Only one horse/rider pair shows at a time, so the judge may focus on every element of the test. Judges never take their eyes off the horse and rider for the entire duration of the test. In order to record scores and comments, each judge has a scribe sitting beside them. As the test is ridden, the judge quietly whispers element scores and comments to the scribe and the scribe writes everything down.

I assumed everyone had memorized the elements of their particular test as I had done. I thought it was required so one would know the pattern of one's test. So I was surprised to see a trainer standing at a mid-point along the rail of the arena, calling out each element to their student throughout the test. How I wished I had known a "caller" was allowed! I would not have the added nervousness of hoping I didn't forget an element of the introductory tests Sam and I were going to ride. As I walked back to where Sam stood tied to our trailer, I told myself, "You've memorized entire recitals of piano music—thousands of notes, dozens of pages, from Bach to Beethoven to Dello Joio. You can handle this!"

Thus fortified with a little positive self-talk, I saddled my beloved Sam.

As we ambled toward the show arena, I noticed a group of riders in a nearby arena, apparently riding in erratic patterns, and all in each other's way. It wasn't until much later I learned that this arena was a "warm-up" arena, where one could go many minutes prior to your scheduled test time, to warm up your horse and yourself and practice. As we approached, the ring steward—the person who makes sure every entrant is ready to enter the show ring—noted the show number I had attached to Sam's bridle and said with no slight irritation, "*There's* number 67. You're up! Get going!"

The ride between the warm-up and the show arena was not very long, but still, I could hear several non-subtle whispers as Sam walked along on a loose rein, his neck stretched out and his nose poked forward. "Who is she, and why on earth would she come to a show like this? And with *that* horse?" "She's not even shaved his muzzle, or clipped his fetlocks!" "And look at his *tail*! Not trimmed or banged!" I took a deep breath, gathered up the reins just a little, and Sam and I moved into position to "Enter at A."

Dressage is a European sport, centuries old, the outgrowth of necessity in training horses to be well-balanced, quick war mounts in the eons before machines. Due to its origin, dressage arenas are built on the metric system, specifically, a rectangle sixty meters long and twenty meters wide. Letters are placed at certain intervals around the perimeter of the arena, to provide points of reference to the rider. "A", situated at the mid-point of one of the twenty-meter "short" sides, is typically where one enters a dressage arena. The opposite short side's mid-point is marked "C", and that is where the judge sits, where he or she has an open view of every aspect of the arena, thus every stride of a dressage test. The mid-points of the sixty-meter "long" sides of the dressage arena are marked "E" and "B" respectively. There are other letters involved, but one can generally get around an arena if you know those four letters and their locations. Oh, yes, and "X". "X" is at the very center of the dressage arena, at the point where a line drawn from "A" to "C" intersects with a line drawn from "E" to "B." At the start of every dressage test (at that point in time, the rules have changed since), the horse and rider must stop at "X" and salute the judge.

Sam's favorite gait was always "standing still" so our first movement of our first dressage test, "Enter at A; at X, halt, salute" was flawless. Sam ambled straight down the center line, and, on perfect cue with slight pressure from my legs and seat, he halted. At X. I gave the judge a sharp salute and took a deep breath, and got ready to "pick up a rising trot." As I gave Sam the cue to move forward and trot, he ignored my leg and seat and, instead, focused on my racing heartbeat and nervous breathing. And, having been my stalwart protective mustang for years and years, and miles and miles of trail riding in the Great Smoky Mountains just the two of us, Sam decided something had frightened his beloved Esther, thus perhaps he should wake up and take note of the unseen demon and get ready to take action.

For a mustang, this means freeze, raise one's head, scan the horizon for any possible threat, and prepare to bolt in the opposite direction. Sam froze at X. He raised his head so high his neck become a straight pencil at a forty-five degree angle, not the rounded, supple, muscular neck so coveted in dressage, with the head softly on the vertical and the horse ready to move forward at the slightest cue.

Sam was cemented to the ground. I did not own, nor ever ride with, a whip or spurs. I could only squeeze harder with my legs and seat, kick Sam in the sides, or talk to him. I squeezed until my thigh muscles began to jump, but still, Sam would not budge. It never occurred to me to take a deep breath and do an instantaneous toes-to-nose relaxation check, knowing (as I do now) that a horse will sense the rider's relaxation and the horse, in response, will relax and go forward.

I only knew my scruffy little sorrel and white mustang was standing at "X" for what seemed like an eternity, and all along the arena perimeter, people were watching and starting to laugh. Had they been laughing at me, I couldn't have cared less. But I could not tolerate the idea of anyone laughing at my beloved Sam.

I don't recall ever kicking Sam. I certainly didn't kick him that day as we stood at "X." Instead, I told myself to treat this like a trail ride. So I spoke softly to Sam. "C'mon, boy. It's just a new place, with a different type of wildlife—human wildlife. And that judge is just like a deer on the Schoolhouse Gap Trail. No biggie. So, c'mon now, let's move forward."

Sam's ears flickered back and forth between me and the judge, who sat straight ahead of us at "C." After a few more moments of immobility, Sam decided to trust me, and off he went, at his shambling trot. Some elements of the test remain a blur to me, because I had no one calling out each element and I was incredibly focused on remembering where to go and whether that element was at the walk or the trot. At that point in time, introductory tests did not include canter as an element.

My mind refocused when we got to the element of our test that called for a "walk on a long rein" diagonally across the arena. "Long rein" translated to "trail rein" in my mind at the time, so as we turned to start the diagonal line, I gave Sam full rein. He understood that to mean that he could meander and take his time, and my legs worked hard to keep him on an unwavering diagonal line, knowing any deviation from the diagonal would cost us points. Somewhere about two-thirds of the way across the arena, Sam spied a green, five-gallon bucket someone had turned over and left just behind the arena rail. In Sam's mustang mind, the green bucket was an unknown and, as such, a thing to be feared until figured out.

He stopped.

His head came up and he glared at the green bucket first from one eye and then, slowly turning his head, from the other eye. His ears were back, just like he pinned them when we were on a trail and he could smell javelinas—the wild pigs that live in the mountains and dig amongst the roots for grubs and such. I could nearly read his thoughts.

Mom, this is not a fun trail ride. We're just going around in this little box, filled with sand. There are strangers all around and they're making all sorts of noise. Worse, there are strange horses all around, and they're all much bigger than me. And there are strange things all around, like that big green round object with the shiny handle. See it? Right there in front of us? I don't want to walk closer to the green thing, Mom. Why can't we just go back out into the woods for a nice, relaxing trail ride like we usually do?

I was embarrassed by the thought of the judge excusing us for Sam's refusal to finish his diagonal, so, in order to get him moving, again I spoke to him in a soft, reassuring tone.

"Sam, it's just a bucket. Just a big, green bucket. It's absolutely nothing to be scared of, okay? Just a bucket, boy."

As between any species, the best relationships are built on absolute trust, and thus it was with me and Sam. Hearing my voice, he immediately knew he could trust me not to guide him where something dangerous might be, so he started walking again, keeping a keen eye on that green bucket. As we turned to head down the center line for our final, "halt/salute," I thought perhaps things had turned out okay, other than the two sticky spots. From my vantage point aboard Sam, I failed to see his outstretched nose. I was used to his shambling trot and oblivious to the disjointed, inharmonious picture he presented from the ground, with his back down, his head up, and no help from his rider to put his body in better balance to carry a person without stressing his back and legs. I was unaware of the idea of "contact," where the horse's forward movement keeps just enough "pull" on the rein that the rider can feel every movement of the horse's head, jaw, even his tongue. Sam always traveled on a loose rein on trail, and our few dressage lessons had not yet changed that.

After leaving the arena, we ambled over to where the Reece family stood at the edge of the arena. They alone had clapped for us upon the completion of our test. I sat on Sam and we watched some of the other "intro" riders. Tall, slim, elegant riders on tall, leggy expensive horses. One bucked and tossed his head; an angry and explosive gesture. One broke into an energetic canter, a gait not included in that particular test. Another refused to stand still during the halt/salute at X.

Back at the trailer, as I untacked Sam and brushed him out, my hopes soared. Surely Sam and I would score fairly high, relative to the bunch of unbroken, unmannered equines I had just watched, despite their impressive pedigrees and wealthy riders.

When the scores were posted, I was surprised to see a white ribbon attached to our scoresheet. Sixth place. Sam and I were the worst of the six intro rides? How was that possible? He had not bucked, nor cantered, nor been impatient and disobedient. He had merely stood longer than he should have at "X" and stopped one time on his diagonal. How had that warranted last place? *Last place! The worst of the lot.*

I scanned our scoresheet, noting comments such as: "Needs more impulsion." "Needs more contact." "Needs more thoroughness from tail to nose." But our riding score was still not abysmal, and I could not imagine the other rides being so much better than ours that we had gotten last place. Sam was worth more than last place. Surely there was some mistake.

Then, at the bottom of the scoresheet, under "penalties," I noted the following comments, the last of which was underlined for emphasis: "penalty: - 2 points; talked to horse." "penalty: - 2 points: talked to horse again." "Rider, note: *you must never speak to your horse while in the arena!*"

Sam had not done poorly, despite his high head and his shambling trot and the unspoken rule of paint-colored horses being highly disfavored in dressage. The mistake was mine. Mine alone. I had failed Sam. I had cost us 4 points. In dressage, the difference between first and last place is sometimes a matter of half, hundredths, or even, in world-class competitions, *thousandths* of a point. To lose *four whole points* for a technical mistake was unthinkable. And unforgivable.

But I had had no idea. Nobody had ever told me not to talk to my horse during our test.

Chapter Thirty-One

Kindness is one of the best gifts beings can give one another, in my opinion, and I have been greatly blessed throughout my life with kindnesses, large and small, bestowed upon me, both by animals like Sam, and by various humans along the journey. There is a large equestrian facility in east Tennessee, River Glen Equestrian Center, and the folks who own and run the place, the Graves family, are some of the kindest folks you'll ever meet. Situated on over 200 acres right along the beautiful Holston River, River Glen is serene and elegant. Bill Graves, his sister Cathy, and their retired parents literally turned an old hog farm into one of the premier show facilities in the southern United States, and, along with nationally-recognized "rated" shows and events, they are kind enough to welcome local riders and their horses to come out and school, hold shows and local club events, etc.

River Glen is such a lovely farm that, when a local dressage show was scheduled to be held there, I decided to take Sam, despite our abysmal outcome at our first show. I knew River Glen would draw some really fine horses, but I figured that even if we didn't do well in the introductory classes we entered, we could enjoy a long, leisurely ride over the beautiful hills and trails of River Glen.

River Glen was constructed to be versatile, so both western and English riding events are held there. For dressage, River Glen can have four dressage arenas going at the same time, plus large, lovely warm-up areas. The place has permanent stalls for 250 guest horses, plus hook-up and parking facilities for horse trailers ranging from modest two-horse bumper pulls to huge tractor-trailer rigs.

I packed up Sam's dressage saddle, a used Giacomini saddle that fit his back like a glove—so I didn't care that it was brown (dressage saddles are traditionally black)—and his English bridle. I also packed his trail hackamore, a bitless headstall with a sheepskin-lined noseband that Sam just loved. He enjoyed our trail rides without metal in his mouth, and I don't blame him for that. I would have used the hackamore during our dressage work, but someone had told me the dressage rules required me to use a bit.

Kindness appeared to me in various forms that sunny Saturday at River Glen. Cathy Graves greeted me warmly when I walked into the secretary's office to pick up our show packet. She made me feel as welcome as if I'd brought some fancy German warmblood, instead of my friend Sam. "You can put Sam in any of the show barn stalls that are empty." I was dumbfounded. Sam got a stall?

"But I can't pay extra for a stall." I said quietly, embarrassed that even $15.00 was too much for my budget.

"There's no charge today," Cathy smiled at me sweetly. To this day, I have no idea if there really was no charge for stalls, or if Cathy decided to give me one for free. But I was so happy to be able to lead Sam off our little two-horse trailer and put him in one of the spacious, airy box stalls at one of the River Glen show barns. The stalls include wrought-iron yoke gates, so each horse can stick his head over the door comfortably and see his surroundings. Within moments, Sam had poked his head through the yoke and was looking all about, up and down the shed row, just like all the finely boned warmbloods and Thoroughbreds were doing. What a lovely sight! My little sorrel-faced riding partner standing in the shaded stall of a proper show barn, free to turn around or do whatever he felt like, instead of being tied to the trailer in the summer sun.

Two local dressage matriarchs, Ann and Sue, noticed Sam in the stall. They came over and greeted us warmly. Whether the results of our first show had made the rounds of the local dressage community, I can't say, but I was tremendously grateful when Ann offered to "call" my test for me this day, and Sue volunteered to videotape my tests. Sam on film! What a wonderful thing! I was delighted and grateful, and, when it was time for our first test, I stepped into the saddle with a happy heart.

Sam and I were entered in two classes, just like last time. Intro A and Intro B. I started to utilize the warm-up ring, but there were several large, well-bred horses trotting and cantering all over the place and Sam was intimidated. So was I, for that matter. So we just walked around the outside edge of the warm-up ring until it was time for us to enter the show ring.

As promised, Ann was standing just outside the ring, at the middle of one of the long sides. I heard her calm, strong voice over the pounding of my own heart.

"A. Enter working trot rising. At X, halt, salute." And so we began.

Ann's voice was a wonderful anchor throughout the test, and I was able to really focus on each element: walk, trot, walk, turn, trot, and on and on. Introductory tests are not very long, but they seem just as long as Grand Prix tests when you're a novice, and Sam and I were as green as grass.

At the end of our first test, I actually heard a few people clapping. It was an amazing feeling, and I reached down and hugged Sam's neck. He hadn't stopped at all. There were no green buckets lying about to arouse his protective mustang instincts. He seemed happy and relaxed, and he stayed relaxed while we stood outside the arena and watched the other competitors in our class.

When it was time for our next test, Ann again called out each element, allowing me to focus on riding my best. I caught Sue filming us out of the corner of my eye, so I knew I'd be able to review Sam's movements at a later time. But as we came to our second and final, X, halt, salute for that day, I knew the results were unimportant. No matter what the outcome, I felt like we had a successful day. Sam had enjoyed himself. And so had I.

We walked out of the ring and I thanked Ann and Sue for their wonderful, thoughtful kindness. Then I rode Sam back to the show barn. I took off his English bridle and put on his hackamore. I mounted up and turned Sam away from the whole show scene, with the high-dollar trainers, well-bred horses, and wealthy owners and riders. As we turned toward the lovely hills that comprise River Glen's cross-country course, with Sam relaxed and unhurried, ambling along on a loose rein, one lovely rider commented, "Well, your horse isn't much to look at, but I must admit I would never get on my horse with just a hackamore!" A backhanded compliment, perhaps, but I took it as a kindness, nonetheless. And with a happy, light heart, my best friend and I headed out on the trail.

Two hours later, as we wandered back to the barns, Ann and Sue came up quickly, with eager looks on their faces.

My Friend Sam

"There you are! We've been looking for you! The scores are in! You need to go to the secretary's office right away!" They were talking so quickly it was difficult to tell who was saying what.

I knew there had been several riders in each of the Intro classes, so I didn't expect Sam to score very high. I was quickly learning the subjectiveness of dressage judging, and paint-colored horses were highly disfavored. Small horses were also looked down on, the current popular trend being dark bay German warmbloods, and the bigger, the better. As I looked around the show grounds, however, I could see that the show was winding down and many folks had already packed up and left while Sam and I were enjoying our ride. So I assumed the secretary was impatiently waiting on me to come down and pick up our score sheets.

I quickly untacked Sam and turned him back into his airy box stall. As I headed towards the secretary's office, I turned and smiled again as I saw his small, sorrel face watching me from his yoke gate. "Someday I'll build you a barn with your own yoke gate, Sam!" I said to him cheerily, and turned and jogged toward the show office.

Sure enough, when I got there, nearly all the tests had already been picked up by other riders, and I felt badly that anyone might be waiting on me.

"I'm so sorry to make you wait; Sam and I went for a trail ride and were having such a good time, I lost track of time!" I looked at Cathy, expecting to be justifiably chastised for being so rude a guest.

Much to my surprise, however, Cathy just smiled and said, "We're not ready to pack up, so don't worry about that. I just thought you'd be eager to see your scores."

I laughed and relaxed a little. "After our last show, which was our first show, I'm not sure I ever want to see another test score sheet again—ever! It was just fun to come out and enjoy your lovely farm, and I'm so grateful to you for letting us come."

"Still, I do have your tests for you," she replied, and the tone of her voice made me suspect that, once again, my test scores were not what I had hoped for.

I was surprised, then, when Cathy handed me a score sheet with a red ribbon attached to it. "Second Place! Sam and I came in second?" I was astounded, and delighted, all at the same time. It seemed unbelievable that we were not absolutely last in our classes again.

Cathy calmly said, "Yes, for Intro B you came in second place. Congratulations!" She seemed as pleased as I was. Then she caught my eye and said, "Your Intro A scoresheet is over there, on the table behind you."

I turned around to pick it up, not caring if we were last place in that test. Sam had earned a second place—a red ribbon! It was a glorious day!

Sitting there, all alone on a stark white tabletop, was our Intro A test result. One sheet of white paper. Yet that was not all. Sitting on top of the score sheet was an etched glass trophy, and alongside the trophy was a blue ribbon. Trophy? Blue ribbon? Speechless, I turned back to Cathy without touching a thing.

"You and Sam not only won the Intro A class, Esther, but your score was a high score. Sam won a trophy!" She was smiling so big, and so sincerely. And then I couldn't see anything because my eyes filled up with tears.

"We *WON?*" I still could not believe my beloved spotted Indian pony had won over those leggy, beautiful horses.

"You WON!" Cathy hugged me, and pressed the score sheet and Sam's blue ribbon and elegant glass trophy into my shaking hands.

My Friend Sam

"We WON!" I shrieked with delight. "We WON! I have to go tell Sam!"

I dashed out into the sunlight and ran all the way back to Sam's stall. Ann and Sue greeted me there, eager to share in my happiness and success. But I only had eyes for Sam.

"You DID IT, Sam! You WON!" His large brown eyes were bright and happy, and even if that was due to the relaxing trail ride he had just enjoyed, I took it to mean that he understood. "You are a GOOD BOY! A GOOD, GOOD BOY!"

Ann and Sue quickly took trophy and ribbon from my shaking hands and I threw my arms around Sam's neck. "I love you, Sam! We did it!"

Chapter Thirty-Two

Sam and I had been inseparable best friends for nearly two decades when we won our first dressage class. Over the years, we had ridden hundreds of miles, just the two of us, with Sam sauntering along in his steady, unhurried walk. This evening I sat, as I often did, on an overturned bucket in the corner of his stall, chatting with him as he contentedly munched hay and kept a soft eye turned in my direction. I told him again and again what a fine horse he was, and what a wonderful friend he was. With Sam in my life, I had everything I had ever dreamed of, or wished for, or wanted.

A horse of my own.

I studied his coat, as I had done countless times before. I loved the contrast of colors: the deep russet and bright white of his overall coat. The black hair core of his tail, surrounded by sorrel strands that formed a thick, wavy waterfall down to the ground behind him. "Your tail is the envy of many dressage horses, Sam." As the evening sunlight filtered through the boards of his stall wall, I could see the single black splotch on his inside right hock, a reminder of his tri-colored paint dam, Kickapoo. I never grew tired of looking at Sam. I never got bored with Sam. I never wanted anything more than Sam.

In that moment, I wished every horse-loving girl in the world could have what I shared with Sam. Not just the blue ribbon or trophy or knowing that, for that test, on this day, we were the best pair in the class. I knew lots of folks who had won ribbons, yet their horse didn't trot up to the fence and whinny every time they drove up. Not just the knowledge that I had a horse and didn't have to lease one or beg others for catch-rides. I knew plenty of folks who leased horses but still didn't seem content. No, what Sam and I shared was something different. Something special. Something genuinely profound. It included mutual trust, but was deeper than trust. It included mutual respect, but was far more personal than respect. It included affection, but was different, somehow, than the affection shared between dog and master. Sam weighed eight hundred and fifty pounds and was easily capable of causing me serious injury or death, should he ever choose to do so. Yet he had always been gentle as a lamb with me, even when he was a green-broke two-year-old and I knew hardly anything beyond the horse-related books I had read as a child.

Sitting there, I recalled how it had taken me quite a long time to locate the American Indian Horse Registry, in Lockhart, Texas. This was back before the internet and no one had ever "googled" anything. I had finally located the AIHR, through some helpful folks at the Kentucky Horse Park, and had verified Kickapoo's AIHR registration. I had thought long and hard about what Sam's registered name should be. I wanted his formal name to describe him perfectly. Despite the fact that the Cherokee were not known as a horse-based Native American culture, I decided Sam's name should be in Cherokee, to pay our respects to the fact that

My Friend Sam

Sam and I lived in East Tennessee on what was once Cherokee land.

I had done some research and liked the idea that most Native American cultures did not use the word "friend" lightly. They allowed time, and events, to show a person's true character before acknowledging the bond that, for many of them, denoted a new brother, irrespective of DNA. For a Native American to call you "friend" is a huge honor, as well as a lifelong commitment to behave as a trusted, cherished and respected member of the family. I had pondered that notion and tried to count my own friends. There were precious few, and I was fine with that.

Sam stopped eating and walked over to me, putting his head in my lap so I could scratch his ears. Wisps of hay stuck out of his mouth on both sides, tickling my arms. His soft brown eyes half-closed in contentment as I rubbed the base of each ear. I leaned my cheek against his broad forehead and closed my eyes, inhaling the scent of my most trusted equine confidante, knowing his name was perfect.

Gi Na Li I Sa Mi. (Key.NAH.lee.ee SAH.mee)

My friend Sam.

I reflected again on how rare it is to be blessed with such a kind, sweet horse. He was surely a once-in-a-lifetime companion. I thought about all the fun animal characters of the James Herriot book series that began with, *All Creatures Great and Small*. I recalled the incredible trio of books about Polar Bear, Cleveland Amory's cat, including, *The Cat Who Came for Christmas*.

"I should write a book about you, Sam." It was a spontaneous thought, but, no sooner had I spoken the words than the idea took on a life of its own. "A book for *children*, Sam. No, wait! A *series* of books! That's it! I can tell the world about how special you are, while teaching children that each one of them is special, too. I'll make them like the *Clifford the Big Red Dog* series, Sam. You'll be famous!"

Sam, the soon-to-be-discovered literary star, ignored the excitement in my voice and went back to eating hay.

"Oh, Sam, this will be great! I'll include various breeds of horses, to represent all the different sizes, shapes and colors of human children. Each one will have its own strengths and weaknesses, so the children who read your books will realize that, no matter what their shape, size or color, *they have value*, just like a Quarter Horse, or a Morgan, an Arab, and a Shire all have value. And we'll include KC the cat!"

It was thrilling to think of immortalizing my beloved Sam in a series of children's books. I wondered if Breyer modeling company might even make a model of Sam someday. How awesome would that be!

I quickly sketched the story line and main characters. Sam, of course, and KC the cat. I had always looked up to Marshall Matt Dillon of "Gunsmoke" fame and Pa Cartwright of "Bonanza" as my idea of what a good man should be. Both characters rode buckskin horses, so I created a strong, buckskin American Quarter Horse named Luke. He would represent all that is the best of the American west and western riding. I had always admired the true story of Justin Morgan and the creation of the Morgan breed, so I created a lovely dark American Morgan horse named Sunny. Small and compact, she would be strong and versatile. I created a beautiful grey Arabian horse and named the Arab Tobruk's Delight after a lovely local Arabian breeding facility, Tobruk Farm. Chris McAdoo, son of the owners of Tobruk Farm, was an artist; perhaps he could illustrate Sam's books for me. I really liked Monique Felix's "Mouse" book series and her illustrations, but I was an unknown person in Tennessee. I knew Ms. Felix would never consider drawing lovely illustrations for my books and, even if she would be willing, I had no money to pay her. But I wanted Sam's books to be beautifully illustrated, so they were as much a joy to look at as they would be—I hoped—to read. I created a big black Shire named Jingles. I had Bonanza's Hoss Cartwright in mind for Jingles' personality—large, a bit clumsy, but totally faithful and loveable.

Somehow, from the very beginning, I saw a series of books. "Sam the Horse" would be the first title, and it would introduce young readers to Sam and all his friends. The second book, "Sam Gets Ready for School" would lead the readers through a grooming session, told from the horse's perspective. Brush in the direction the hair grows. Put the saddle on with the stirrups up so they don't whack the sides of the horse as the saddle settles into place.

I grew up in Tennessee, home to the beautiful Tennessee Walking Horse, and, tragically, home to many horrible abuses of this wonderful, kind breed of horses, as well. I wanted to teach children to be kind and thoughtful to horses, and to consider every interaction with a horse from the *horse's* point of view.

Change one mind, change the world. Right?

Surely, the least I could do was try.

Chapter Thirty-Three

I didn't know much about legal matters at this point in my life, including intellectual property. But I read up on such things as "work for hire" in copyright law and made sure to have Chris McAdoo, the artist for Sam's books, sign off his rights under the "work for hire" rule. I created a trademark for Sam's logo, "Sam the Horse" and had it registered. At the time, I had no idea if Sam would totally flop, or be the next "Snoopy" or "Garfield," and I figured, better safe than sorry. So I tried to think ahead and plan for success.

I sent numerous letters with my manuscripts to all the major publishers of children's books, like Scholastic and Golden Books. In return, I received dozens of rejection letters.

Chris and I worked and worked on trying to get the drawings as I had envisioned. I wanted the softness and fine detail of Monique Felix. I had seen some of Chris' pastel portraits of horses, and he certainly had the right skill set to create lovely artwork for Sam's books. Chris' interpretation of Sam and his friends, however, was more in a caricature style. I wanted to respect his artistic interpretation, but the artwork never really reflected what I saw in my mind. But I ran out of money and couldn't change the drawings again, so, in the end, only Luke really reflected the soft, realistic essence of my vision for the books.

My beloved friend, Doris, finally decided enough rejection letters had come my way, and, in her typical, gracious style, surprised me out of the blue one day.

"I want to help you get your books published," she said. And, with that, the "Bank of Doris" became my venture capital and the books went to a private press for printing. We started with a run of 1,000 each for "Sam the Horse" and "Sam Gets Ready for School." I had obtained ISBN numbers for the books, and, once they were published, Ingram—the largest book distributor in the United States, which happens to be located in Tennessee—decided to distribute them.

Doris and I were ecstatic when the first orders from Ingram's came in. They wanted hundreds of books at a time, and soon we were back at the printer to order a second run of 2,000 for each title. I could hardly believe it! I was a published author and Sam was going to be a sensation!

I shipped books and thought of all the creative ways we could market Sam. I envisioned Sam backpacks and lunchboxes and maybe even, like Snoopy and Garfield, a Sam cartoon. The sky was the limit, and each time I spent time with Sam, I gave him an update and discussed our big plans.

"Sam, we've shipped the entire first printing and had to order more books!"

"Sam, I think I'll send a copy of your books to Breyer modeling company and see if they want to make a Sam model!"

"Sam, I've got another book idea—'Jingles Gets a Christmas Tree'—what do you think of that title?"

And then one day, somehow, word had spread with the press, and the phone rang. "Sam, you're gonna be on *television!*"

I had a few bright yellow t-shirts made up, with Sam's new trademarked logo embroidered on them. Sam got scrubbed until his white patches glistened like sunlight on snow. I put on the sunny yellow t-shirt and my best jeans.

And Channel 10 News came to film my beloved Sam for a local interest feature show, "Life at Five."

I was nervous during the interview, but when the cameraman asked me to walk with Sam, it felt like the entire universe stopped, as it always did when I was with Sam. I spoke to him softly as the camera crew trailed along right behind him or beside us, taking a tight shot of Sam's feet and getting the crisp, 'clip clop' of his freshly shod feet on their audio.

When the segment aired, I regretted not being more relaxed, but I was so incredibly proud of Sam! Surely this was the beginning of great things for us!

"Sam! Davis-Kidd booksellers called! They want to hold a premier book signing! I'm going to read your books to children, Sam, and then sell them and sign them, too!"

"Sam! Barnes and Noble called! They want to host a book signing—and they want *you* to come!"

Taking a horse to a book signing takes a good bit of organization. I bought a portable, collapsible corral for Sam, not only so he could move about freely, but also to keep people from crowding him. I bought a garbage can and filled a bucket with cat litter, in case Sam had to go to the bathroom. Hay and water had to be packed. I used the bed liner from my pickup as a rubber mat so Sam would not slip as he stood in his corral, just outside the front door of Barnes and Noble.

A horse outside a bookstore is difficult to ignore, and Sam drew a crowd. Adults tended to stay back, as ladies fussed about their manicures getting dirty or some such. But the children! Oh, the children *loved* Sam! They encircled his portable corral and stretched their arms toward my best friend, calling, "Sam! Come here, Sam! Over here, Sam! This way, Sam!" And Sam, with his wise eye and kind heart, slowly walked around the corral on his own, letting each and every little hand stroke his nose, his neck, his side or his flank.

I stayed in the corral with Sam, a pen in my pocket, and when someone purchased a book, I would autograph it without leaving Sam's side.

"Sam! The Dogwood Arts Parade called! They want us to be in the parade!"

"Sam! There's a Native American pow-wow coming to town; they called and they want you to be there!"

Since Sam was a registered American Indian Horse, I felt we needed to do something special for the pow-wow event. I read where Native Americans used to notch the ear of their favorite warhorse to mark the animal as special or sacred. While most Indian ponies remained in a herd near camp, favored war mounts were kept near the warrior's lodging, both to protect the horse from theft and to denote its station as a member of the warrior's family. When the prized mount left this earth, often warriors would cut off part of their mane or tail, in order to keep some the horse's spirit with them in this world and allow it to pass on to their next great mount. Some warriors felt such a brotherly bond with their war mount they would cut off their own hair and braid it into the horse's mane, so the horse would know that a part of the warrior's soul traveled with the beloved horse to the Spirit World.

My Friend Sam

I would never have notched Sam's ear, but I liked the idea of somehow marking him as special to me and a member of my family. My maternal grandmother's surname, Roberts, traces through Revolutionary War times, including ancestor soldiers who fought for American freedom from British rule, back into ancient annals of Scottish history. Roberts is a sept of Clan Donnachaidh, the clan known for protecting Robert the Bruce when he fought to free Scotland from England. The clan crest is a powerful fist upholding the crown of the Bruce. The clan tartan is a lovely, understated plaid on a deep blue background. I registered with my clan some years ago.

I decided to use a beautiful wool scarf woven in my clan tartan around Sam's neck to mark Sam as my special horse for the pow-wow. I also found some brightly colored cedar berry beads, strung by the Navajo, and made Sam a necklace. He didn't seem to mind wearing the scarf or the berry necklace.

Tourists who came to the pow-wow seemed delighted to meet Sam and we had an enjoyable time there. Sadly, however, I was unaware of many restrictions and traditions associated with Native American culture; while the organizers had invited Sam and me to be there, the actual Native American participants were disgusted with the inaccuracy of having an Indian pony at a pow-wow in the Cherokee region. Had we been in Comanche territory, Sam might have been welcome, but here, he was not. I, being of Scottish descent, was unwelcome under any circumstances, and the Native American people made me aware of my "outsider" status in their unfailingly dignified way.

I have great respect for the Original American Peoples, and greatly regret the many injustices they have suffered for generations. So while I was honored to bring Sam to that

Esther L. Roberts

particular pow-wow, we never accepted another invitation to a Native American gathering. I was unwilling to allow anyone else to handle Sam, and I could not change the fact that I am not Native American.

Chapter Thirty-Four

Other local and regional stores—toy specialty stores, tack stores, elementary schools—called and wanted Sam to come to book signing events. We traveled so many weekends to so many places I lost count. I wish now I had kept better records. Various friends helped at all the events, and I was grateful to each of them for their assistance. Then came the day Waldenbooks from Atlanta called.

"Sam! Waldenbooks in Atlanta wants you to come! To the *mall*, Sam!"

I used leather pads and wrapped Sam's feet with bright blue Vetwrap, a removable veterinary bandage wrap, to make sure Sam didn't slip on the polished marble floors of the indoor shopping mall. We had to walk through a high-end department store in order to get to the Waldenbooks, which was located near the mall food court. The petite makeup artists, each one in her stiletto heels and crisp black lab coat, stared in disbelief as Sam navigated around all the elegant cosmetic and fragrance stands like Chanel and L'Oréal, past the upscale purse and jewelry displays, with his coat gleaming and his tail brushing the floor with a soft "swish, swish" with every stride. I was so proud of my friend Sam at that moment!

The mall was two stories tall and the food court included an atrium to the roof. Hundreds of children were screaming Sam's name and the cacophony of sound was deafening. Sam paused outside his portable corral and cocked his head, turning one large, dark eye toward the glass roof of the atrium, while his other eye took in the long line of children who were waiting to pet him. Then he dropped his head and nudged me in the small of my back, compelling me forward into the corral, as if to say, "Okay, I'm ready. Let's do this!"

Four hours later, after every child had been introduced to Sam, the star of the *Sam the Horse* children's book series calmly walked back through the mall, gentle as a lamb, showing absolutely no signs of fatigue or impatience, despite the chaos of the afternoon.

Driving home from Atlanta was a glorious trip. At the time I was driving the big Ford F-250, and that powerful gas 460 pulled Sam's little two-horse bumper-pull Merhow trailer like it was nothing. Sam was always an excellent traveler, so I knew he was contentedly munching hay or dozing. The only time Sam grew anxious about traveling was backing out of the trailer. When I bought the Merhow, I made sure it had a ramp so Sam would not have to back off into thin air; he, like so many horses, really didn't like the idea of a "step" trailer and preferred the ramp attachment. But he loaded easily and traveled well.

For myself, the miles flew by while my mind ran wild with possibilities. I thought of Garfield, and Snoopy, and Clifford the Big Red Dog. Sam could be as popular as any of them! He was a horse, and a spotted Indian horse to boot, so he should enjoy a broad audience and wide-ranging appeal. I made plans for stuffed toys and backpacks and sleeping bags, all with Sam's signature coat colors and patterns. Perhaps a plastic model of Sam, even!

Once home, I wrote a letter to Breyer modeling company and enclosed a set of Sam's books. Naively, I failed to talk with an attorney beforehand. Had I done so, I would have realized that, by sending Sam's books without any agreement between me and Breyer, I had given Breyer a very valuable idea, which they shortly produced in the form of a generic Indian Horse, followed by several others, eventually including the American Indian Horse Registry's now-famous stallion, Rowdy Yates. I never heard anything from Breyer. I never contacted them nor considered bringing suit against them, either. Why? Well, for starters, it was my own ignorance that gave them the idea of making model Indian ponies, if it was, in fact, the receipt of Sam's books that gave them the idea. And, second, the end result was exactly what I had hoped to achieve in the first place (other than making Sam a Breyer, of course). The American Indian Horse Registry and original mustang horses, have garnered lots of good press and attention from Breyer's production of these models, including Rowdy Yates. Good for Rowdy, and for his owners. I am sincerely delighted for them. I hope Breyer, and other model makers, continue to produce model Indian horses and mustangs so new generations will be made aware of these marvelous horses.

For me, it was never about making tons of money. The only reason I wanted to make a living from Sam's children's books was to give me more time to write, and more time for Sam. The main reasons for Sam's children's books was to share quality information with children about how to treat horses with kindness and to show children that horses, like children, come in various shapes, sizes, colors and with different skill sets. I wanted to encourage children to focus on maximizing their own abilities without making negative comparisons between themselves.

In the end, my motives proved self-supporting, because one day, a couple of boxes of unsold books were delivered back to me. "What is going on?" I thought.

I contacted Ingram's book distributors, and only then learned that, while bookstores can order numerous copies of books, they also have the right to *return* all the books if they don't sell in a given period of time. I was stunned. Over the next several weeks, more boxes arrived. Each box included not only the unsold books, but also a "credit" invoice where Ingram's was deducting from the royalty payments the cost to them of each unsold book. The numbers were scary, and I was ashamed to tell Doris that the return on her investment was dwindling quickly to zero. As the weeks progressed and the books kept coming, I was mortified to have to tell her we were now in the red.

Doris is a brilliant businesswoman, and a kind soul, which is a rare combination in my opinion. She wouldn't have risked putting the money into the books if she hadn't had the money to lose, so she took the news calmly and with great graciousness.

The third book in the series, "Sam Goes to the Show" has yet to be illustrated or printed. Other books in the series, such as "Jingles Gets a Christmas Tree," and "Luke Goes to Oklahoma" all wait for the right opportunity to be published and sold. There are no Sam backpacks, nor sleeping bags, nor stuffed toys. Yet.

Chapter Thirty-Five

May of 2001 was a time of celebration and hope for me and Sam. Sam was comfortably boarded at Crosstie Stables. I had bought a singlewide trailer in a gated mobile home park located less than two miles from Sam. It wasn't the same as having enough land to have Sam at home with me, but it was good enough until I could save enough money to buy my own place.

Law school graduation was in May. I was starting a brand new job as an attorney in June. I had received more than one offer of employment, and I was grateful for each. In the end, however, I chose to follow in my grandfather's footsteps.

Due to the loss of vision in one eye as a boy on his family's farm, Grandpa was unable to serve in the United States military. He had, however, worked at the Oak Ridge National Laboratory complex, long before the government entity overseeing the place was called The Department of Energy. When Grandpa had worked there, it was the Atomic Energy Commission that ran the place. Now, the Department of Energy, or DOE, was in charge, and DOE Oak Ridge was hiring one attorney. A patent attorney, to be exact.

For all three years of law school, I had assumed I would become a trial attorney. I had clerked at a local insurance defense firm and learned a great deal about this area of legal practice. The cases were typically difficult, emotionally. When a young mother driving a small car with three children inside decides to race a train, the train can take no evasive maneuvers except slam on the brakes, and stopping a freight train is, literally, like trying to stop a freight train. Or a carload of college youths traveling to spring break in a car with slick tires on the interstate. Rain comes, tires hydroplane, tractor-trailers are also on the interstate. Tragedies happen, and big carriers like train companies or trucking corporations must pay damages. The legal system tries to make certain those damages are fair, both to the victims, and to the companies. It's a tough business to try and equalize all the competing interests.

The job at DOE, on the other hand, seemed incredibly interesting and challenging. I would be writing patents on cutting-edge inventions arising out of research funded by the U.S. government. I would be a public servant, just as my grandfather had been decades before, when he was a physicist/chemist at the lab. As a public servant, I would not make the salary I might as a private attorney, but I would certainly make more than I had ever made as a piano teacher.

I liked the idea of knowing every citizen was my client, from the CEO of billion-dollar companies to Tony, the retired Navy man who worked third-shift at the local gas station. I liked the idea of working with inventors and getting to stay connected in some way to a creative process. I was going to miss my music career greatly, I knew. One of the best aspects of going into government practice was the idea of relatively steady hours. At last, I would have a reasonable income, reasonable hours, and evenings and weekends free to spend with Sam.

I wanted to share the joy of graduation day with my friends, family, and Sam, too. The Moirs graciously offered me the use of Crosstie, so we set up a huge white tent in the front paddock and had a big, catered barbeque cookout for everyone to enjoy. I turned Sam loose in the paddock as well, and everyone enjoyed getting to relax, eat, and spend time together, while Sam meandered amongst everyone, grazing here or there and generally acting like the oversized dog he was. Sam was now twenty-eight, still strong and healthy, and I was looking forward to finally being able to relax and enjoy giving him anything he needed.

It had only taken twenty-six years.

Chapter Thirty-Six

September 11, 2001 was a gorgeous day in East Tennessee. I drove to Oak Ridge, as I had been doing since starting my new job in June of that year. I am a morning person and like to start the day early, so I enjoyed watching the sunrise during my morning commute each day. I thought of Sam and how he must be enjoying the cooler temperatures after a typically hot summer. I knew I would drive over and see him that evening, as I did every evening. Given the bright, sunny sky, I looked forward to a leisurely ride together through the trails within the lovely wooded hills of Crosstie Stables.

I was sitting at my computer at the Federal Building in Oak Ridge that morning, checking email and scanning various news webpages for the headlines of the day, when an alert flashed from cnn.com. A plane had struck one of the World Trade Center towers. Across the hallway was a conference room that contained a television, so I walked over there and turned on the news, wondering about the details. I figured some pilot of a small plane had lost control or had a malfunction.

I watched in horror as the second passenger jet struck the second tower. I knew then the United States was under attack. I had been a federal employee for only twelve short weeks.

I thought of Oklahoma City and the bombing there back in 1995. The World Trade Centers were not federal buildings, however, so I was uncertain as to whether we would be evacuated or what would happen. I had no idea what would be expected of me, but I prayed for courage and asked God to give me strength and to take care of Sam, no matter what happened to me.

I observed the management at Oak Ridge move rapidly, collecting data and coordinating the security of the Oak Ridge National Lab and the Y-12 Nuclear Weapons Complex. Everyone was grim and determined to protect Oak Ridge. The problem was, no one knew what to expect, when or where to expect it, nor how many more planes might be plowing into buildings. We were informed that all air space was to be cleared and all planes grounded.

Then the Pentagon was struck by a plane. I was numb and unable to turn away as the conference room television showed the South Tower collapse, and, just a few minutes later, the North Tower followed suit, imploding in smoke and fire to the ground. It was utterly inconceivable to me that my beloved country, that the United States of America, could be so vulnerable.

Word came from Washington: All federal facilities were under immediate and indefinite lock-down; all nonessential personnel were to evacuate immediately. I had taken both the Tennessee and Oklahoma bar exams in July, but would not know my bar results until October. As such, I was merely a law clerk, not yet even an attorney. Certainly, I was nonessential. And so, while those critical to security were moved to a secure command center, I and many others were told to go home and not come back until further notice.

My Friend Sam

I drove directly home, absolutely terrified that other planes might defy the coast-to-coast grounding order and plunge from the sky. I remember looking out the windshield of my truck every few seconds, trying to be prepared for evasive maneuvers if a plane appeared. But the skies over East Tennessee remained calm, cloudless, and clear of enemies.

I went inside my trailer long enough to change clothes and hug Lizzi Mae, my large tabby and white cat. Then I drove to Crosstie. Sam was grazing, utterly unconcerned about terrorist attacks or international politics or anything of the sort. The sense of normalcy at Crosstie was a great comfort to me that day. Still, out of an abundance of caution, I led Sam to his stall and we spent the day together there in the big white barn that defines Crosstie. I sat on the threshold of his stall while he dozed with his head over the thin chain that stretched across his stall door. Sam never tried to get out, so one chain was all it took to keep him in his stall. A few other boarders came around, and John, Libbi and Butch were there, but all in all, it was a very quiet day. I didn't want to hear any more news. I didn't want to see any more images. Like everyone else who had watched the events of that morning unfold via television, I had watched people climb out of a massive skyscraper and jump to their death. I had heard the unforgettable sound of human beings hitting the ground. I had watched perfectly good airplanes being *intentionally* flown into buildings. For what purpose? Whose soul could be so dark as to wish such massive harm on innocent strangers? It was beyond comprehension, and I chose to try and block out the awful sounds of that morning with the welcome, comforting sounds of Sam munching on hay or lazily whisking a fly with his tail. This, along with

Esther L. Roberts

the warm sunshine and soft sounds of the wild birds in nearby trees, gave me great comfort throughout that tragic day.

Chapter Thirty-Seven

By November 11, 2001, while the U.S. government was still working to respond to the September 11 attacks, my individual life was back to normal, overall. I was working to learn my new job, understand management and chain of command within a government framework, and generally feeling intense pressure at work. I had passed both the Tennessee and the Oklahoma bar exams. I had taken the U.S. Patent Bar exam but had not yet received my exam results.

November eleventh was a crisp, sunny autumn Sunday, and Sam and I enjoyed a relaxed afternoon ride. Crosstie Stables includes numerous pastures, each with its own character. Some are open, grassy meadows. Others are wooded, rolling hills. One pasture is bordered along one side by a wide creek. In some places, the creek runs through wooded gorges, and you ride along the top of the ridge through dense trees, where you can look down at the creek and all the waterfowl that call it home, including various species of wild ducks and elegant blue herons. In other places, the land flattens out, the trees become sparse and the creek broadens to a calm expanse where beavers build dams and raise their young. More than once, Sam and I had ridden by the creek and been happily startled by the sharp slap of a beaver's tail on the water. Deer and wild turkey live in these secluded sections of Crosstie. It is a tranquil and beautiful place. The ground alongside the beaver dams is firm and safe; it invites a rider to canter a bit, and today was no exception.

Sam and I came down off the wooded ridge and he responded readily when I asked for a faster gait. Unusual this day was the fact that the herd of horses who resided in this field also joined us for a run. These horses included those whose owners opted not to pay for a stall in the barn, so the horses lived outside in this relatively remote pasture, or they were young stock not yet ready to ride, or senior horses who had been retired to a life of leisure. The one common thread to all of them is they were not handled much, and they could be a rough and rowdy crowd at times.

So this day, as Sam picked up the canter, I was a bit wary as we found ourselves surrounded by the herd. Alongside Sam's red and white mane were chestnut, white, and black manes flowing in the wind as we all ran together. I thought of pulling Sam up to let the herd pass, but with so many horses behind him, I decided that would be unsafe. The herd began to take on its own momentum, and the horses rushed all around us. Sam and I were pelted by clods of dirt thrown up by the pounded hooves of these horses, running for the sheer delight of their freedom. As the herd began to pass us, one animal cut away from the herd and stayed alongside Sam. I watched as this horse, a young black filly, carefully matched her pace to Sam's own somewhat stilted canter. The filly could obviously outrun Sam, for she sometimes bucked a stride or lashed out at Sam and never fell behind, but rather, stayed directly alongside Sam's right shoulder. She had the look of devilment in her eyes as she pinned her ears flat against her finely shaped head, snaked her long neck out and nipped at Sam. Something about the filly seemed vaguely familiar, but I didn't have time to ponder who she was or when I had seen her before. I was far more concerned with keeping Sam under control as she pushed into him and tried to turn him with her own body. I was afraid both horses would stumble and we'd all go down in a heap, but Sam seemed amazingly calm and steady, despite the abuse he was getting from the ebony tempest that ran alongside him. I glanced down at Sam's face, and was amazed to see his eye steady on the filly. I had never seen that look in Sam's face before. I had no idea what it meant. As I gradually slowed Sam, the filly seemed annoyed with the slower pace, so, with ears pinned and mane flying, she lashed out at Sam one last time, her heels soaring higher than his ears, so high could she kick, and then she bolted off to catch up with the herd and leave us to ourselves. The rest of that ride was calm and relaxing, and Sam seemed very content to return to his stall. When I gave him a final pat goodnight, the Moirs were starting their evening rounds, and I knew Sam would be fed shortly, and all was well.

The next morning, November 12, Libbi Moir called me at work. "Sam didn't eat his grain last night, and he's not showing any interest in grain or hay this morning." Sam had never missed a meal in his life, so I was concerned, but not overly so.

"We had quite a run with the herd out back yesterday, Libbi. Maybe he's just a little stressed."

"Well, that's probably it, but I wanted to let you know."

When my workday was over and I drove over to see Sam, he seemed fine. He just wasn't hungry. I didn't ride him that evening, however, just in case he needed the rest.

On Tuesday, November 13, Sam still had not eaten, and his bowel movements were getting loose, more like a cow patty than the normal horse apples. I called Eric Martin, DVM, and he met me at the stables after work. Normal temperature for a healthy horse is around 99-101 degrees. Sam's temperature was 103. "He's getting dehydrated, Esther. We may need to give him some fluids." That scared me. Fluids meant putting Sam in the hospital.

Wednesday, November 14, I drove to work as usual. I had asked Eric to come and see Sam that morning. Eric called me at work. "His temperature is 104, Esther, and his bowel movement is now liquid. He needs fluids, and we need to get his temperature down." That evening after work, I hooked the trailer to my truck and went to get Sam from his stall.

The change in Sam was shocking. His eye seemed distant, as though distracted by some inner pain. His long, beautifully thick tail and his white legs were now stained from diarrhea. He loaded easily and we drove to the equine hospital where Eric worked. It was a small facility out in the countryside, but the care was state of the art. I walked Sam into a large, well-lit and well-ventilated stall. "It's okay, Sam," I soothed, as Sam looked around the unfamiliar surroundings. "I realize it's not your regular home, but it's just for a few days, until you get to feeling better." I turned to Eric. "It's just a bug, right? Nothing too serious, right?"

"We need to work aggressively to get his temperature down." Eric's tone told me he had genuine concern. "I don't know what's causing the issues, Esther, but I want to run some tests."

I held Sam's head steady while Eric shaved a place on his neck and inserted what looked to be a huge needle. Eric explained as he worked. "We need to help Sam flush out his system and rehydrate, so I'm going to put fluid into him as quickly as he can take it, thus the large needle." Soon, a horse-sized bag of IV was hung suspended over Sam's head, with a rotating hanger which follows the animal's movements. Unless the horse rolled, they would never get tangled in the IV line.

Thursday morning, when Eric called me at work, I knew the news was not good. "His temperature is still at 104, Esther, and the diarrhea has gotten much worse." I drove to the hospital Thursday evening, and Sam was irritably sloshing his muzzle about in a water bucket, but not drinking anything. I noticed the IV hanger now held four bags of fluids, all of which were coupled together and running directly into my beloved friend. And running directly out, as well, apparently—Sam's tail was a soggy mass, and putrid-smelling yellow liquid flowed constantly from Sam's bowels.

"I'm not sure what the cause is, Esther, but I do know, from the test results, that Sam's kidneys and bowels have completely shut down. His body is not filtering anything out, so he is basically poisoning himself with the unfiltered waste. We keep pumping fresh fluid in with all these IVs, but his temperature and all the test results stay the same—still high fever, obvious infection, and no functioning filtration system."

"Do you have any ideas what might be wrong? I mean, I just rode him on Sunday, and he was absolutely fine!"

"It could be something he ate, like molded hay. It could be one of the illnesses that are starting to invade Tennessee, such as Potomac fever or West Nile virus. Whatever the cause, if we don't get it under control soon . . ." Eric paused to make sure I understood, "Esther, if we don't get this under control soon, Sam won't make it."

I remember looking at Eric as if I'd never seen him before, despite the fact that we had years of veterinarian-client trust built between us. It was completely incomprehensible to me that Sam might not live to be an ancient horse. He was a small horse, so his expected lifespan was perhaps thirty-five to forty years old. I had no delusions about riding him that long; indeed, my former riding instructor and I had speculated that, one day, when Sam was ready to retire, I would look for a finished schoolmaster gelding who could teach me dressage. I liked bay horses and had often shared with Sam my dream of getting him a big, bay brother, so he could laze around during his older years and make the bay boy do all the work.

Now, however, six months out of law school and Sam only twenty-eight, I was nowhere near ready to consider retiring him or replacing him as my primary riding partner. The notion that he might soon be gone from this world was so utterly foreign to me, I was numb at the very thought.

"Esther, Esther!" Eric's voice cut through the fog of my rambling thoughts. "Do you need to sit down, Esther? You've gone really pale."

"No. No, I don't want to leave Sam." I watched as the stream of foul-smelling yellow liquid continued to stream down Sam's tail. I had thought his body was ridding itself of infection; I had not realized his life was draining from him in a steady stream of infection.

"Esther, we're doing all we can, and he's had a good life..." Eric tried to comfort me, but I was having none of it.

"Don't give me platitudes about his 'good life,'" I snarled. "We've been living hand-to-mouth for *twenty-six years*! Only *now* am I finally getting to a place where I can buy whatever Sam needs and not have to worry about it. Now! And now you're telling me he may not make it? That simply can*not* happen!" My shock was so genuine, I absolutely refused to believe I was watching Sam's decline.

My Friend Sam

I wanted to stay with Sam overnight, but Eric would not allow me to. And my job with DOE was still so new I had not accrued much leave time, and I needed to work to pay the veterinary bills that were mounting exponentially, day by day and moment by moment.

On Friday morning, Sam's temperature was still at 104 and the tests showed the toxicity of his blood was climbing steadily. I got to him as quickly as I could after work, and Eric met me with the latest test results. Still insanely high fever; blood toxicity nearly off the charts. At least the workweek was finally over and I could devote the entire weekend to Sam. I had told no one at work about Sam's illness, nor his hospitalization. Who could be expected to understand that my best friend, my own heart and soul, the very creature which defined and inspired me, was gravely ill? To most outsiders, Sam was "just a horse," or "just a pet," or they would, like Eric, urge me to consider Sam's age and maintain a reasonable perspective. I was unable to have any perspective but the one Sam had given me: twenty-six years of stunningly loyal, completely trustworthy, absolutely *perfect* friendship. How could anyone expect a rational response to such a loss? How could I possibly consider living the rest of my life without Sam?

Chapter Thirty-Eight

I walked into Sam's stall Friday night, with Eric offering a steadying hand. I felt like I was looking at a horse I'd never seen before.

His paint coat was the same pattern, but otherwise, Sam was a complete stranger to me. His head was down and he was listless and lethargic. His spine protruded along his back and his ribs were beginning to show. The despised yellow fluid streamed constantly out of Sam, soiling his tail, his backside, and his hind legs, defying the hospital staff's best efforts to keep both Sam and his bedding clean. The yellow river was running faster than they could keep up.

Sam's entire abdomen was bloated and distended, like some grotesque cow's udder that badly needed milking. "It's due to the kidney failure," Eric explained.

Over Sam's bowed head, four IV bags flowed as fast as possible. Eric's voice was quiet in the evening stillness. "We've given Sam thirty gallons of fluid today, Esther."

The magnitude of Sam's illness finally hit me. Thirty *gallons*. And still Sam had lost almost three hundred pounds in three days.

I spent a long time with Sam, trying to search his eye and hear his soul, but that evening, he remained distracted and often stood with his eyes closed, fighting the battle within.

Saturday morning, November seventeenth, I arrived at the veterinary hospital early in the morning. Eric was already there.

"Temperature is still 104. The toxicity tests from this morning are maxed out, Esther. Sam is getting worse, not better."

Looking at him, I could see the continued decline evidenced in Sam's demeanor and his posture. He was weary of the battle, and it showed. He didn't even try to lift his tail anymore, but rather let the yellow diarrhea flow in an unstoppable stream. His abdomen was turgid with the fluid his kidneys could no longer filter out.

As I stood in the stall, numb to the core, Eric's voice continued, as gently as possible. "One way, or the other," he began slowly, "Sam will not survive this weekend, Esther. He is too far gone." I didn't respond, other than closing my eyes and hugging Sam's neck, careful to avoid the IV lines. "There is something you have to consider, and deal with, Esther." He paused, and I finally opened my eyes, feeling as listless and broken as my beloved friend Sam.

Eric's voice was gentle, despite the harsh reality of his message. "Burying a horse is no small task, Esther, and you have no land. Have you thought about what you'll do with Sam?"

I could not speak, but simply shook my head. No, I had not considered where to bury Sam. I had not considered last Sunday that by this Sunday he would be dead.

"I know it's not an easy thing, Esther, but you have to think about it. It's the weekend, and you're going to need a backhoe."

My Friend Sam

I don't remember leaving Sam's stall that Saturday. I recall it was around lunchtime, but I wasn't hungry and never thought of food. I called the Kentucky Horse Park, thinking I could haul Sam's body up there and have him buried near Man O'War. The lady on the phone kindly informed me that all horses except Man O'War were buried, "in the manner of Thoroughbreds: we accept the head, heart and hooves and bury them together. You can place a marker on the grave if you wish."

The idea of dismembering Sam made me absolutely nauseous, and I quickly hung up the phone.

I drove to Crosstie. It was a beautiful November Saturday, and the place was bustling with activity as folks were grooming and saddling horses or untacking after finishing a morning ride. Perhaps Eric had called Libbi. More likely, Libbi just knew. Either way, she met me at my truck and, with her typical grace and insight, didn't say anything more than what was required.

"You know you're like family, Esther, and so is Sam. You pick the place; we'll take care of the details."

I felt on the verge of tears but didn't want to cry in front of all the other boarders, some of whom were young girls who had Sam's books and thought of Sam as a famous celebrity. It would break their youthful hearts if they knew Sam was fading away.

"Backhoe," I whispered to Libbi. "Eric said I'll need a backhoe." It never occurred to me that, having run a professional boarding stable for years, this was not the first equine burial the Moirs had organized.

"I know, Esther. You just pick the place, anywhere on the whole farm. Don't worry about anything else."

I think I said, "thank you." I hope I did. I honestly don't recall.

Chapter Thirty-Nine

I left the barn and all the folks behind me and began walking out into the pastures of Crosstie. I avoided the popular trails so I wouldn't run across any riders. I didn't want even well intentioned inquiries as to Sam's health. As I headed up one of our favorite hills into the woods, the tears began to come.

I'm not a big crier, and I'm certainly not a public crier, and I learned from my paternal dna that audible crying brings on more punishment. So at this moment, when my entire soul was breaking into a million unmendable pieces, I wept silently. The tears flowed so intensely I could not see. My nose ran so much I could hardly breathe. And yet I kept walking.

I found what I sought in the second field, up high on a hilltop that is partially wooded. It would never flood. It would have plenty of sunshine for warmth and yet the trees all around would protect it from inclement weather. I didn't think about the fact that Sam would not again bask in the sunshine, nor need protection from the elements. In my mind, I was finding the best outdoor spot for Sam I could, and I knew it when I saw it, despite the constant onslaught of tears. And yet I kept walking.

I couldn't seem to stop walking, and I don't know why. Perhaps stopping would allow all my feelings to catch up to me. Perhaps stopping would mean the only thing left was to either wait for Sam to die or, worse yet, find myself backed into the corner of having to make that decision for Sam. So I kept walking.

My vision was so blurred with tears that I didn't realize when I came upon the herd of horses in the back field by the beaver dam. I just kept walking, oblivious to the sounds of their hooves stomping at flies or the occasional snort. Normal horse sounds. Healthy horse sounds. I never heard them. I angrily brushed the tears away, time and time and time again, but they would not stop. I had never cried so hard, nor so much, in my entire life. I had no clue how to deal with Sam's impending death. We had lived so much of life together, how does one continue on alone?

As I stumbled along, blinded by tears, I heard hoofbeats behind me. I ignored them at first, thinking my mind was playing tricks on me, imagining Sam was once again happily plodding along behind me. I received a sudden nudge in my back, however, and I could hardly ignore that. Without turning around, I realized one of the horses from the herd had followed me and pushed at me, and I reached behind me and swatted at its muzzle, missing it entirely but still hoping to convey the message—"Leave me alone."

The beaver pond was a blur of tears and I walked on into the woods near a place where a spring brought fresh water out of the ground. As I approached the spring, I was again nudged from behind. I winced as the sharp, bony nose hit my spine, and I turned around, determined this time to send the stray, whoever it was, back to the herd. I was absolutely broken and could not be bothered right now! Didn't this horse understand that? Whoever it was, *it was not Sam*, and therefore, it was of no consequence to me that day.

I turned around to face the nuisance and immediately froze. Standing behind me was the black filly that had given Sam such a hard time last Sunday. On what was, although I had no way of knowing it at the time, Sam's and my last ride together. Of all the horses that called Crosstie Stables home, I wondered why on earth, on this day of all days, I had to be bothered with this unwanted, unbroken, wild thing. She walked around in front of me, turned to face me and blocked the path with her body. I was wary, knowing that, even though she didn't look to be more than two years old, she was still big enough and strong enough to hurt me if she took the notion. But as I stopped and looked at her, I realized she had no malice in her soul. She wasn't there to hurt me. She was there to—*what*? I could not believe what I saw in the filly's eyes. There was kindness in those huge black depths. I saw a wisdom that belied her youth.

Confused, I sat down and studied her at length. The crest of her neck and dish-shaped muzzle, her short back and overall refinement, all told me she had a good deal of Arabian blood in her veins. Her every movement was elegant; indeed, one might expect to see her likeness alongside some textbook definition of "grace."

Yet here was no calm gelding, but a mare, and a young one, so who knows what mood swings she would be capable of? Here was no trained schoolmaster, but a totally untrained animal of tremendous power and tempestuous spirit. It was inconceivable that I should even consider such a thing, especially at this moment in time. Yet I saw something almost indescribable in her eyes. More than a question, it was—an offer?

I spoke to her then, and asked her one question, out loud, in English. "Do you have any idea the size shoes you're offering to fill?" The question was hardly spoken before the black filly began moving. Slowly, steadily, she walked to me and dropped her head, pushing her muzzle into my lap. Total submission. Completely unbidden. Insanely unexpected.

Every horse has its own scent, and the black filly didn't smell anything at all like Sam. She stayed with me as I dried my tears in her mane. She walked along behind me until I reached the gate into the next field, and then she turned and walked back toward where she had left the herd.

Chapter Forty

As I slowly trudged back to the barn, emotionally overwhelmed and exhausted, I simply prayed for the strength to survive. Libbi was waiting for me, and, as always, she was kind. "Eric called; Sam's about the same. Eric said tomorrow..."

The grim reality set in. "Tomorrow, then." The tears were gone, thankfully, and I knew it would be a very long time before I wept again. Now, it was time to deal with the situation and do whatever I had to do to take the best possible care of Sam, as I had always done, for twenty-six years.

I asked Libbi about the black filly. Who owned it. How much did it cost. Libbi seemed puzzled. "What black filly?"

"The black blaze-face in the back field. Looks to be about two years old."

"Yes, I know the one you're talking about. I'm just surprised you don't remember her. She's Rachel's daughter. The one born in the stall behind Sam's stall two years ago. The one you always said you were glad you didn't own, because she is so spirited and wild!"

"So, who owns her now and is she for sale? If so, what's the price?"

"What happened out there, Esther?" So I explained to Libbi that, despite my plans to take my time and mourn Sam and then, maybe, someday, think about buying that big bay schoolmaster everyone dreams of, the black filly had separated herself out from the herd, came to me and picked me.

"Well, if she picked you, we both know that's a very rare and special thing. She's definitely your horse, at least in her own mind. And she's so full of fire, it wouldn't do anyone any good to try and convince her otherwise." Libbi was a wise horsewoman. She continued.

"The black filly is mine, Esther. Rachel's owners didn't want the baby, so they gave her to me. She's been out back for two years because I had no idea what I was going to do with her. But if you want her, I know she'll have a great home with you, so she is yours."

Libbi thought for a moment and then added, "Since we don't know what made Sam so ill, I'll have Butch sanitize his stall tomorrow. It will be ready for the black filly by tomorrow afternoon."

Had the entire week not been so traumatic, I would have been repulsed at the notion that Libbi was already talking about Sam in the past tense, but, given that the entire week was so surreal, it just didn't register with me at the time.

Chapter Forty-One

Sunday morning, November 18, 2001, dawned clear and crisp. I considered what the day would bring and I knew I wanted to keep some part of Sam with me. Relying on what little I knew of Native American history, I braided a section of my hair in a slim, tight braid. It was an underside layer, so no one would notice when I hacked it off. I dressed in my best shirt, jeans and boots. I wasn't sure why, it just seemed like the appropriate thing to do. I grabbed a couple of plastic bags and my best pair of scissors and, with a set jaw, climbed in my truck—alone. My sister knew Sam was very ill, as did a few other people. But today was to be as private as possible. Today was all about Sam.

I drove to Crosstie early, grateful to find the place deserted. It was too early for most folks to be out and about on Sunday. With leaden hands, I hooked my trailer to my pickup truck, knowing I would be bringing Sam's body home later that day. How I hoped he would spare us both the decision that loomed on the horizon of the day. But, as I thought about that, I became afraid that he might leave before I could say good-bye, so I hurried to the hospital as quickly as I could safely haul my rig.

Sam was not only alive when I got there; he was standing up and looking alert! Despite being thin and dirty from the diarrhea, his eye was full of life and he walked to the stall door to greet me when I arrived. I am a firm believer in miracles, and I was positively delighted to see him.

Eric was there, and we were both surprised to see Sam up and focused again on the outside world. "He's getting better, Eric!" I was thrilled. Eric, however, was far more cautious. "I'm not sure of that, Esther. Often animals, like humans, seem to rally just before they leave us." I had never heard of such a phenomenon.

"No one can explain it, really. But many people, and some animals, tend to seemingly get much better right before they pass on." Eric pointed to Sam's still turgid abdomen and steady stream of liquid that continued to drain from Sam. "We're nowhere near out of the woods on this, Esther."

"May I take him out for a short walk, please? Maybe some fresh air will do him good."

"Go ahead. It will give me the opportunity to clean the stall again. Just be careful if he gets unsteady on his feet and starts to go down."

Blissfully happy, I put Sam's halter on him, attached his lead rope, and carefully led him from his stall. He was very game to try and walk, and I tried to ignore the swaying, drunken steps Sam took in his weakened state.

We walked out into the sunshine and greeted the bright autumn morning. The leaves on nearby trees were lovely shades of yellows, reds, oranges and browns, and birds and squirrels darted among the branches. Sam watched them with interest, and he seemed to be happy to stand in the warm sunshine. Moments passed as Sam and I enjoyed the beauty of the morning together. Off in the distance, the bells

My Friend Sam

of a small country church chimed the start of the Sunday morning service.

As the sound of the bells faded, Sam dropped his head and stared at me. Always obedient when on the lead line, today he turned of his own accord and started pulling me back to his stall. As we walked along, I felt him become unsteady under my hand as it rested on his shoulder. He turned and walked into his stall, and gently collapsed onto the stall floor.

Eric was there and we both knelt over Sam. As Eric checked his vital signs, he said, "It won't be long, Esther. I'm so sorry."

Sam lifted his head into my lap, and his eye told me how very tired he was. He could not have said any plainer, "We shared a lifetime of perfect friendship. We even enjoyed this morning and made a few final, happy memories together. Now, please have the courage to do for me what I know you would want me to do for you, were our positions reversed."

I never took my eyes off Sam and Eric said, "We can let him pass here, Esther, and then drag him into the trailer, or," he paused to help me realize what he was asking permission to do, "we can do this another way." The idea of letting Sam suffer any longer, and then dragging my beloved pet's body to the trailer and somehow stuffing him inside seemed the least dignified thing I could possibly do, so I closed my eyes and shook my head. Eric understood.

As he left to get what he needed, I took the scissors and cut my hair. I entwined the braid of my own hair with some of Sam's mane while he lay with his head in my lap and his eyes closed. Then I took the scissors and cut off most of Sam's mane. I leaned over him, oblivious to the stench of his illness, and cut off some of the hairs of his tail. I put his mane and tail hairs into the bags I brought along for this purpose, knowing that someday, at the right time, I would make a memorial for Sam and have some part of him with me always.

Eric came back to the stall, and quietly knelt down. "Esther, I want you to go into my office and wait there. I need to get Sam up, and that may not be pleasant to watch." Numb, like an obedient child in the midst of trauma, I rose and started to walk away.

A few steps later, I stopped and turned and ran back into the stall. "Wait!" I fell down beside Sam and lifted his weary head one last time into my arms, holding him close and kissing his forehead. "Thank you, Sam. Thank you so much for every moment of twenty-six perfect years. I love you. I'll miss you every single day between now and when we see each other again. Thank you for being my friend, Gi Na Li I Sa Mi. My Friend, Sam."

Chapter Forty-Two

Eric assured me Sam maintained his nobility and kindness, getting up on his own and loading like the excellent horse he was. When I walked out to the truck, the trailer was closed up tight.

I drove back to Crosstie, grateful to arrive before the after-church crowd showed up for a Sunday afternoon of riding and conversation. This time, however, I did not stop at the big white barn. This time, I put my pickup in four-wheel-drive and drove straight up the hillside into the protected sunny spot. I left the trailer doors closed, telling myself that Sam was already gone and the rest was just matter—inconsequential molecules that needed to be buried but did not house my beloved friend.

I had brought along three songs to play in the truck audio system, my private funeral service for my beloved friend. Rod Stewart singing, "Have I told you lately that I love you?" The song was perfect for my relationship with Sam. "Fill my heart with gladness; take away all my sadness; ease my troubles, that's what you do." I had never once laid eyes on Sam and not smiled. Ease my troubles, indeed. Celin Dion's beautiful voice singing, "I'm everything I am, because you loved me." I thought of every life decision I had made where Sam had been my first concern. My relationship with Sam had literally come to define me. And, last of all, Vince Gill singing, "Go Rest High on that Mountain. Son, your work on earth is done." And so it was.

I waited alone for hours, sitting on the wheelwell of the closed trailer. I didn't mind. Those hours, indeed, helped me come to realize that some grief is so profound it cannot be shared and it cannot be healed. Like warriors who lose their legs in battle. You don't get new legs. Even if you get prosthetic legs, they're still not the same as your own legs. You learn to cope without your own legs.

I believe life is like a tapestry and relationships are like unique threads within the tapestry. Folks enter your life and that color thread starts becoming woven into the fabric of your being, your history. Then they leave, and that color begins to fade out of the day-to-day weaving. My life tapestry had twenty-six years of the bright, beautiful color of Sam. Now, that thread was gone forever. I might weave with a different thread, but it would never be the thread of Sam.

The backhoe arrived around sunset, along with Butch to help bury Sam. Butch made sure Sam's body was enshrouded in blankets, so I would not see his lifeless face. I was grateful for Butch's care and concern. I did reach down and touch one of Sam's front feet, right at the hairline. His body was cool to the touch, and that told me he was truly gone. It was only after this assurance that I allowed the backhoe to start pushing dirt upon my beloved friend.

After the last scoop of dirt was packed down on the grave, I climbed into the cab of my pickup and drove slowly back to the big white barn.

The light in Sam's stall was on. Butch had scrubbed the stall walls, floor, buckets and feed bin with antiseptic. There was a deep layer of new bedding, pine shavings that smelled clean and fresh. A pile of hay was in the corner and the water buckets were filled. A new halter and lead rope hung on the peg outside the stall door. Thanks, Libbi, for your steadfast thoughtfulness.

I picked up the halter and lead rope and walked out into the darkness, wondering if I would even find the black filly, let alone would she allow herself to be caught. As I walked, I wondered, *Why, Sam? Why her? She's so spirited! I'm not sure I can handle a horse like her! She's hardly two, and doesn't know a thing...*

In the back field, out of the darkness, the black filly with the blaze face again separated herself out of the herd. She walked right up to me, and put her muzzle into the halter, just like Sam would have done. I softly patted her neck and said, "I had no idea you would come into my life at this particular time. I haven't considered owning another horse, let alone a mare, and a young one. I don't even have a name for you! And I have to be honest, I'm so dreadfully numb from Sam leaving that I don't know how much use I'll be to you for a while. Maybe a long while. Maybe you'll just be a pasture ornament. I have no idea. I have no idea where this is going..."

As we walked together back to the barn, for her first night in a stall since she was weaned, the answer to my question came to me, as though Sam could speak for the first time.

She is young and untrained, just as I was when our journey together began, Esther. Yes, she is spirited, but you've had twenty-six years to learn how to harness that spirit without breaking it. This is why she is the next horse for you, and why you are the only right owner for her. You will teach her, and she will inspire you...

Esther L. Roberts

Snug in Sam's stall, I gently removed the halter from that refined face as calm, intelligent eyes looked back at me. I walked out of the stall and closed the door behind me, as the words came, unbidden, "Goodnight, Lady Grace."

Epilogue

Perhaps great joy and great sorrow must go hand-in-hand. I only know this: sharing my life with Sam for twenty-six years was the greatest joy I have ever known; burying my best friend was the greatest sorrow I have ever experienced. Yet if such sorrow is the price to be paid for knowing such unspeakable joy, I would gladly do it all over again.

My hope for every person who reads this book is that you, too, may experience the greatest joys life holds in store for you. And, of all the innumerable lessons Sam taught me, my steadfast prayer is that each and every one of us will learn this lesson, and teach it, well:

Be kind.

Esther L. Roberts

Esther is a writer, musician, horsewoman, lawyer, teacher, and animal advocate. Her primary life goal is, "to share kindness and joy everywhere and with everyone." She lives in the foothills of the Great Smoky Mountains in Eastern Tennessee, where she shares her farm with Lady Grace and several other horses, cats, and many wild animal neighbors.

www.ingramcontent.com/pod-product-compliance
Lightning Source LLC
Chambersburg PA
CBHW021400290426
44108CB00010B/318